Main Dish Soups

READER'S DIGEST

MAIN DISH SOUPS

FREDERICA LANGELAND  PHOTOGRAPHS BY JIM KOZYRA

Reader's Digest

The Reader's Digest Association, Inc.
Pleasantville, New York • Montreal

Acknowledgments

In addition to my immediate family and their friends who patiently tasted and critiqued these recipes, I would like to thank the following people for their suggestions, their contributions past and present, and their unflagging encouragement at all times: Gregory David; Anne-Marie Hostache; Bill Krause; Dianne Langeland; Deb Proctor; Joan Tall; and my sisters, Suzy and Carol, both of whom sent me my first soup suggestions in a far-off time and place.

A READER'S DIGEST BOOK

Prepared and produced by
Michael Friedman Publishing Group, Inc.

Editor: Nathaniel Marunas
Designer: Lynne Yeamans
Production Director: Karen Matsu Greenberg
Photography Director: Christopher Bain
Prop sourcing and styling: Sylvia Lachter
Food preparation and styling: Lisa Homa
Photographer: James Kozyra

Reader's Digest Project Staff
Editorial Director: Fred DuBose
Design Director: Elizabeth Tunnicliffe
Project Editor: Martha Schueneman, CCP
Editorial Manager: Christine R. Guido

Reader's Digest Illustrated Reference Books
Editor-in-Chief: Christopher Cavanaugh
Art Director: Joan Mazzeo
Director, Trade Publishing: Christopher T. Reggio

Copyright ©2000 by Michael Friedman Publishing Group, Inc.

Library of Congress Cataloging in Publication Data

Langeland, Frederica.
    Main dish soups/Frederica Langeland; photographs by Jim Kozyra.
        p. cm.
    At head of title: Reader's Digest.
    Includes bibliographical references and index.
    ISBN 0-7621-0266-7
        1. Soups. 2. Entrées (Cookery) I. Title.

TX757 .L29 2000
641.8'13—dc21   99-047394

Reader's Digest and the Pegasus logo are registered trademarks of The Reader's Digest Association, Inc.

Printed and bound in England by Butler & Tanner Ltd.

C O N T E N T S

INTRODUCTION

Homemade chicken soup is the very metaphor of motherly love, the panacea for all the afflictions encountered beyond the parental threshold. It is the first sustenance I can even contemplate eating after a bout of flu, and every winter there is a small stash of chicken stock in the back of the freezer that is strictly off-limits to the cooks of the family (who might use it as stock for their own recipes).

Unfortunately, homemade soup has taken a back seat to the canned variety, much of which is incredibly high in salt content, yet low in true flavor. There is no denying the convenience factor of commercial soups, and there are some tasty ones available, but they will never equal your own efforts in the kitchen. They will not use up the bones from your Sunday roast; the meat tends to

be overcooked, the fish rubbery, and the vegetables soft. In short, a can of soup will never be exactly to your taste. By all means, keep some basic canned soups on hand. Broths can serve as the basis for your own soup pot, and a few basic creamed varieties help build quick, satisfying casseroles. But for a soup that truly satisfies, take the extra time and make it from scratch.

Traditionally, soup has occupied only two places in the meal: the first course and the main course. As for its role as an appetizer, in the words of Reynaud de la Reynière, the soup is to the dinner as the portico is to a building. As the first course, it must be concocted in such a way as to do justice to the feast, somewhat as the overture of the opera announces the subject of the work. In other words, the soup must

prefigure the meal, complementing but not outshining the main course.

Such lofty sentiments do not apply when soup is the main course. But even in this case, there is tradition to consider. Historically, a French *soupe* was not a smooth liquid concoction now referred to as a *potage*. It was a broth based on meat or vegetables, in or with which something else, ranging from simple slices of bread to meats and vegetables, was served. This is part of a hearty peasant tradition, along the lines of New England boiled dinner, pot au feu, or even turkey stew with dumplings.

Finally, there is the latest arrival to the soup family, the dessert soup. Do not underestimate the power of such a sweet punctuation mark to bring a satisfied smile to the lips of every guest at your table.

ACCOMPANIMENTS AND GARNISHES

Bruschetta • Garlic Bread • Croutons

Cheese Quenelles • Chicken Quenelles • Cream Cheese Tartlets • Dumplings

STOCKS AS BUILDING BLOCKS

Chicken Stock I • Chicken Stock II • Chicken Consommé • Beef Stock

Beef Consommé • Vegetable Stock • Fish Fumet

PART ONE

THE
BASICS

ACCOMPANIMENTS AND GARNISHES

The saltine has become the de facto partner to soups in today's dining, but there are many delicious sides that are very simple to prepare and yet add immeasurably to the soup-eating experience. What follows is a collection of recipes for a variety of basic accompaniments that are well-suited to many of the soups in this book.

BRUSCHETTA

SERVES 4 TO 6

INGREDIENTS

1 loaf Italian bread, fresh or otherwise

½ cup (125ml) olive oil

1 clove garlic, coarsely chopped

¼ teaspoon salt or seasoned salt

1. Preheat the oven to 400°F (200°C).

2. Cut the Italian loaf into 3- or 4-inch (7.5–10cm)-long chunks. Cut each chunk in half lengthwise, horizontally to the bottom of the loaf.

3. In a blender or food processor, combine the olive oil, garlic, and salt and process until smooth.

4. Coat one side of each slice of bread with the mixture and toast on a baking sheet in the oven for 5 to 10 minutes, or until lightly browned.

COOKING TIME

15 minutes

TEST KITCHEN NOTES

BRUSCHETTA WAS ORIGINALLY A WAY TO RENDER PALATABLE BREAD THAT WAS GOING STALE BY TOASTING IT LIGHTLY IN THE OVEN, THEN BRUSHING IT WITH OLIVE OIL OR DRIZZLING OIL OVER IT. THIS IS A SLIGHTLY MORE DEDICATED TREATMENT.

THESE DAYS, WHAT IS SOLD AS BRUSCHETTA IS TOPPED WITH A MIXTURE OF CHOPPED ONIONS AND SEEDED, DICED TOMATOES. IF YOU DO DECIDE TO TOP YOUR BRUSCHETTA WITH SUCH A MIXTURE, CONSIDER CUSTOMIZING IT FURTHER BY ALSO ADDING YOUR FAVORITE FRESH HERBS; BASIL, OREGANO, CILANTRO, AND PARSLEY ALL WORK WELL. WITH OR WITHOUT TOMATOES, BRUSCHETTA IS AN EXCELLENT ACCOMPANIMENT FOR SOUPS.

GARLIC BREAD

INGREDIENTS

1 loaf crusty French or Italian bread
1 clove garlic
½ cup (100g) salted or unsalted butter,
    melted
Pinch cayenne pepper, optional

1. Preheat the oven to 400°F (200°C).

2. Slice the bread thick or thin, to taste, crosswise and on a slight diagonal, but do not cut all the way through the loaf. This will keep the bottom crust intact to catch the dribbles. Make a boat of aluminum foil that encases the bottom and sides of the loaf.

3. Peel and roughly mince the garlic, then crush the bits thoroughly with the flat of the knife. Stir the garlic pulp into the melted butter. For a little heat, try adding a pinch of cayenne. With a pastry brush, lightly brush the exposed top and sides of the loaf with butter, then drizzle or brush the remaining butter between the slices. Place on a baking sheet in the oven for 5 to 10 minutes, or until nicely toasted on top and heated through. Serve immediately.

COOKING TIME

15 minutes

TEST KITCHEN NOTES

THE THING TO REMEMBER ABOUT GARLIC IS THAT A LITTLE BIT OF IT GOES A LONG WAY, PARTICULARLY WHEN UNADORNED BY A SEA OF SAUCE OR OTHER MITIGATING FLAVORS.

CROUTONS

INGREDIENTS

1 loaf French bread, preferably
    a baguette
½ cup (125ml) olive oil
1 clove garlic, optional
1 tablespoon mixed dried herbs

1. Preheat the oven to 400°F (200°C).

2. To make cubes: Slice the bread in half lengthwise. Brush the slices of bread lightly with olive oil (which can be infused with a crushed clove of garlic or dried herbs, if desired). Cut the two pieces of bread into ½-inch (13mm) cubes, then toast the cubes on a baking sheet in the oven until golden brown, about 15 minutes, shaking or stirring the croutons occasionally to ensure even toasting. If you didn't add herbs to the oil before toasting, you can shake the still-warm croutons in a bag with some finely chopped fresh herbs.

To make sliced bread croutons: Cut the bread crosswise into ½-inch (13mm) slices. Brush the slices lightly with olive oil, then toast on both sides in the oven, about 15 minutes. The slices also may be shaken with herbs. To impart a delicate garlic flavor, rub the toasted slices lightly with the cut edge of a clove of garlic sliced in half. This is a subtle method that yields a milder garlic flavor than the garlic-infused oil method.

COOKING TIME

15 minutes

TEST KITCHEN NOTES

CROUTONS COME IN TWO BASIC FORMS: SMALL CUBES OR SMALL SLICES OF BREAD, FROM A BAGUETTE. THEY ARE USUALLY TOASTED IN THE OVEN, BUT YOU ALSO MAY PREPARE THE CUBES AND SLICES BY FRYING THEM IN FLAVORED OIL. BE WARNED THAT THIS PROCESS IS HARDER TO CONTROL: IT TAKES MORE OIL AND MAKES GREASIER CROUTONS THAT ALSO TEND TO BE LESS EVENLY TOASTED.

QUENELLES

Cheese Quenelles

INGREDIENTS

5 slices white bread

½ cup (125ml) milk

½ cup (60g) grated cheese
(Parmesan, Cheddar, etc.)

1 tablespoon (15g) butter

2 eggs

2 to 3 cups (500 to 750ml) Chicken
Stock II (page 16), for poaching

1. Soak the bread in the milk, then place in a strainer and press out the milk. Reserve 1 slice.

2. Process the cheese and butter into a smooth paste either in a blender or by pounding in a mortar. Add the eggs and 4 slices of the bread and mix thoroughly.

3. Roll this paste between your palms by teaspoonfuls into sausage shapes the thickness of a little finger. If the paste is too sticky to work with, add the reserved bread; a lot depends on the type of bread you use. Blunt the ends of the quenelles to make them neat.

4. Drop the quenelles a few at a time into simmering stock (the variety of which will vary according to the soup you're serving)—exuberant boiling will make them disintegrate. The stock should be deep enough for them to submerge; when they rise to the surface they are done, about 5 minutes. Remove with a slotted spoon and drain on paper towels or on a clean cloth.

COOKING TIME

5 minutes

TEST KITCHEN NOTES

QUENELLES CAN BE MADE IN ADVANCE AND KEPT IN THE FREEZER. TO MAKE FISH QUENELLES, SUBSTITUTE ½ POUND (250G) FILLETED WHITE FISH FOR THE CHICKEN IN THE NEXT RECIPE. SERVE QUENELLES IN HOT BROTH OR TOMATO-BASED SOUP WITH A SPRINKLING OF CHOPPED FRESH HERBS: DILL, PARSLEY, CHIVES, OR CILANTRO.

Chicken Quenelles

INGREDIENTS

5 slices white bread

½ cup (125ml) milk

¼ pound (125g) skinned, boned
chicken breast, minced

1 tablespoon (15g) butter

2 eggs

⅛ teaspoon salt

⅛ teaspoon ground nutmeg

½ cup (60g) lightly toasted bread
crumbs

2 to 3 cups (500 to 750ml) Chicken
Stock II (page 16), for poaching

1. Soak the bread in the milk, then place in a strainer and press out the milk. Reserve 1 slice.

2. Process the chicken in a blender with the butter, or put it through a meat grinder twice, then mix with the butter. In a separate bowl, thoroughly incorporate the eggs into the butter-and-chicken mixture, then add 4 slices of the bread, salt, and nutmeg.

3. Roll the paste into sausage shapes by the teaspoonful between the palms of your hands, adding the reserved bread if the paste is too sticky to work with. Blunt the ends of the quenelles to neaten.

4. Roll the quenelles in the toasted bread crumbs before dropping a few at a time into simmering stock. Do not allow the stock to boil vigorously. When the quenelles float to the surface, they are done; scoop out with a slotted spoon and drain on paper towels or on a clean cloth.

COOKING TIME

5 minutes

CREAM CHEESE TARTLETS

INGREDIENTS

8 ounces (250g) cream cheese

1 egg

¼ teaspoon salt

1½ teaspoons (7.5ml) sour cream

Dough for a single pie shell,
    any unsweetened type

Paprika

1. Preheat the oven to 400°F (200°C).

2. Mix the cream cheese, egg, salt, and sour cream together until smooth.

3. Roll out the pie dough fairly thick—about ⅓ inch (1cm). Cut out 10 to 12 2½- to 3-inch (64–76mm) rounds. Place these in tart molds so that there is a rim of pie crust to contain the filling; or pinch up the edges and place the shells on a lightly greased baking sheet. Put a generous tablespoon of the cream cheese filling in each tartlet and sprinkle each with a little paprika. Bake for 10 to 12 minutes, or until golden.

COOKING TIME

10 to 12 minutes

TEST KITCHEN NOTES

IF YOU KEEP PIE CRUST IN YOUR FREEZER (IT WILL KEEP FOR UP TO 1 MONTH) OR DOUGH IN YOUR FRIDGE (GOOD FOR 1 WEEK), THESE LITTLE TARTS WILL BE THE TASTIEST "FAST FOOD" YOU'LL EVER EAT. BESIDES ACCOMPANYING *BORSCH* (PAGE 76) AND *SHCHI* (PAGE 73), THEY ARE WELCOME WITH DRINKS, AS AFTER SCHOOL SNACKS, OR EVEN FOR BREAKFAST.

DUMPLINGS

INGREDIENTS

1 egg

⅓ cup (80ml) milk, approximately

1 cup (140g) flour

1 teaspoon baking powder

½ teaspoon salt

1. Break the egg into a cup measure; add enough milk to make about ½ cup (125ml) of liquid. Beat together in a bowl.

2. Sift together the flour, baking powder, and salt. Stir gently into the egg-and-milk mixture. The batter should be stiff, but you may add a judicious spoonful more of milk if you think it necessary.

3. About 10 minutes before the soup of your choice is done, drop the dumpling batter by tablespoonfuls into the soup; the dumplings should not quite touch. Cover with a tight-fitting lid and simmer for 10 minutes, turning the dumplings over after 5 minutes. Serve at once.

COOKING TIME

10 minutes

TEST KITCHEN NOTES

TRY ADDING CHOPPED CHIVES OR YOUR FAVORITE FRESH HERBS AS YOU STIR IN THE FLOUR. OR ADD 2 TABLESPOONS OF FRESHLY GRATED PARMESAN OR SHARP CHEDDAR CHEESE, OR EVEN A TOUCH OF BRUISED CARAWAY OR CUMIN SEED.

STOCKS AS BUILDING BLOCKS

The building blocks of soup are the basic stocks made from vegetables, fish, fowl, or meat; they are to your bowl of soup as the foundation is to a house. The subtleties and complexity of your soup are deepened by the broth behind it. Canned beef stock, consommé, bouillon cubes, and chicken stock are readily available, quick solutions when a recipe calls for stock and you have none on hand, but fish fumet is another matter—I have yet to find it at the grocery.

You may use either cooked or raw meat and bones for your stock, but be aware that if a sparkling clear broth is your aim, you should avoid mixing cooked and raw meats. Also avoid the detritus from smoked meats (unless, indeed, the smoky flavor is a desirable element for your soup) and charred or blackened bits of meat. Mutton and lamb bones will tend to overpower all other flavors; use them only when that is the meat in your soup, as in Scotch broth.

Vegetables are essential to any stock, but there are some to be avoided: peas and parsnips are too sweet and heavy; the darker green parts of celery may be too strongly flavored; and tomatoes are very acidic and should be used with care. The cooking water from vegetables should be added to your stock or soup with an eye to appearances. Water from beets, tomatoes, and dark greens may not be desirable except in very specific cases. Let me put in a good word for the lowly turnip, or rutabaga, a super-vegetable in the world of stocks. Not always a popular vegetable on its own, the turnip bolsters and blends flavors, providing great depth to vegetable and meat stock. Do not forget the turnips.

Finally, herbs and seasonings should be administered with a miserly hand: half a bay leaf here, the stalks but not the leaves of parsley there; whole peppercorns, yes, but only the tiniest pinches of other peppery matter, like cayenne. If you are using dried herbs, tie them in a square of muslin to make them readily extractable at the end of cooking. Salt only very lightly, particularly if you plan to reduce your stock; it is easy enough to adjust the salt content at the end of the cooking process.

The easiest way to degrease your stock is to chill it; the grease will rise to the top and harden there. This coating also serves to seal off the stock and it can be left as it is until you need it. Store it for several days in the refrigerator or months in the freezer. Simply lift off the layer of grease when you are ready to use the stock. If time is short and you can't wait for the chilling process, let the stock rest until the fat rises to the surface, then spoon off what you can, or remove it with the help of a baster. Small globules may then be lifted by applying an oleophilic brush, or with the aid of a paper towel rolled in a tube. Touch the rolled tube of paper towel to the fat, then tear off and discard the greasy end; repeat until the fat is gone.

CHICKEN STOCK I

INGREDIENTS

3 pounds (1.5kg) raw chicken bones,
　　carcasses, parts, and giblets
Cold water to cover, about 2 quarts (2L)
6 thin slices fresh ginger root

1. Break down any whole or bulky carcasses so that they may be readily covered with water. Add the water and ginger root. Bring very slowly to a boil; cover and simmer for 1 to 1½ hours or until all the meat has fallen from the bones.

2. Strain off the stock, discarding the solids. Allow the stock to cool, about 30 minutes. The stock may be kept in the refrigerator for several days (or in the freezer for months), sealed naturally by its layer of fat; or you may skim off the fat and store the stock in the freezer in 1-cup (250ml) containers for convenient access to a reasonable quantity. This stock will be clearer than one made with herbs and vegetables, but you may nonetheless wish to strain it through a dampened, wrung-out cloth before storing.

3. If you wish to reduce the stock before storing it, return it to the pot after straining and boil, uncovered, until reduced by half. Reducing the stock makes good sense because it will be used primarily as a recipe ingredient rather than as a soup on its own; make sure to mark containers of concentrated stock as you may want to dilute it with equal parts water when you use it.

Do not salt the stock until you finish reducing, if at all.

COOKING TIME

1½ hours

COOLING TIME

30 minutes

REDUCTION TIME

up to 30 minutes

TEST KITCHEN NOTES

THIS BASIC RECIPE IS DELICIOUS AND STRAIGHTFORWARD. THE HINT OF GINGER MAKES IT A VERSATILE BUILDING BLOCK FOR A VARIETY OF SOUPS, IN PARTICULAR THOSE OF MANY ASIAN CUISINES.

Chicken Stock II

YIELD: 4 TO 6 CUPS (1–1.5L)

INGREDIENTS

3 pounds (1.5kg) raw or cooked chicken
    parts, giblets and carcasses, cut up
Water to cover, about 3 quarts (3L)
1 carrot, peeled and halved lengthwise
1 small turnip, peeled and halved
1 or 2 stalks celery with leaves
1 onion, halved
1 small bay leaf
1 or 2 stems parsley
6 or 8 peppercorns
2 teaspoons salt

1. Rinse the chicken parts and place in a stock pot with the vegetables and seasonings. Bring slowly to a boil over medium heat, then reduce the heat and simmer until the meat is falling off the bones (about 1½ hours, from start to finish).

2. Strain through a colander, discarding the chicken bones. The vegetables may be puréed and stored for the thickening of future vegetable-based soups. Allow the stock to cool, about 30 minutes, then chill about 2 hours. The fat will rise to the surface, where it will constitute a natural seal until you lift it off.

3. Before using, strain again through dampened, wrung-out cheesecloth or muslin to remove the deposit that will form at the bottom of the container. Adjust the seasoning if using at once, or store in the freezer and season as you use the stock.

4. If you wish to reduce the stock before storing it, return it to the pot after straining and boil, uncovered, until reduced by half. Reducing the stock makes good sense because it will be used primarily as a recipe ingredient rather than as a soup on its own; make sure to mark containers of concentrated stock as you may want to dilute it with equal parts water when you use it.

Do not salt until you finish reducing, if at all. Store in the freezer in 1-cup (250ml) containers.

COOKING TIME

1½ hours

COOLING TIME

30 minutes

CHILLING TIME

2 hours

REDUCTION TIME

30 minutes

TEST KITCHEN NOTES

THERE ARE AS MANY RECIPES FOR CHICKEN STOCK OR BROTH AS THERE ARE THRIFTY COOKS. THE STOCK MAY BE MADE FROM CHICKEN CARCASSES AND PARTS, INCLUDING THE GIBLETS, COOKED OR RAW, OR FROM A WHOLE CUT-UP CHICKEN. BEFORE BOILING, FOR A RICHER FLAVOR AND COLOR, YOU MAY BROWN THE PARTS OF A WHOLE CHICKEN IN BUTTER, OIL, OR CHICKEN FAT. YOU MAY SIMMER YOUR STOCK WITH THE "USUAL VEGETABLES" AND A BOUQUET GARNI OF YOUR FAVORITE HERBS, OR YOU MAY SIMPLY TOSS IN A LITTLE SALT.

THIS RECIPE YIELDS AN EXCEPTIONALLY CLEAR BROTH, WHICH MAY BE REDUCED BY HALF AND STORED IN SMALL CONTAINERS IN THE FREEZER FOR SEVERAL MONTHS. IT MAY THEN BE USED AS IS OR PARTIALLY OR WHOLLY RECONSTITUTED, DEPENDING ON THE DISH IT WILL BE USED FOR.

CHICKEN CONSOMMÉ

INGREDIENTS

1 chicken, about 3½ pounds (1.75kg),
    with giblets

1 onion, peeled, stuck with 1 clove

1 carrot, peeled

1 small turnip, peeled

1 stalk celery with leaves

1 bay leaf

1 teaspoon salt

10 cups (2.5L) water

3½ pounds (1.75kg) chicken carcasses,
    necks, feet, etc.

1. Cut up the chicken and place it with all the other ingredients in a deep pot with the water. Bring very slowly to the boil and simmer for 30 to 45 minutes. Skim as necessary.

2. Preheat the oven to 425°F (220°C).

3. While the stock is cooking, lightly grease or spray the bottom of a roasting pan. Spread the chicken parts and carcasses in it and roast until lightly browned, about 30 to 45 minutes. Be careful not to burn them or your consommé will taste charred.

4. Remove the breasts and legs from the stock; bone these pieces of meat and set the meat aside for other uses. Return the bones to the stock.

5. At the same time, add the browned carcasses from the roasting pan to the stock pot.

6. Add a little water to the roasting pan; heat it gently, lifting and scraping off the browned bits and juices. Add these bits to the stock pot. Simmer for 2½ hours longer with the pot only partially covered.

7. At the end of about 3 hours total cooking time, remove the consommé from the heat. Strain the stock, discarding the bones and vegetables, then strain again through a damp cloth. Allow the stock to cool for about 30 minutes, then chill for about 2 hours. Remove the fat and then clarify (page 124 for directions), if you so desire.

COOKING TIME

3 to 3½ hours

COOLING TIME

30 minutes

CHILLING TIME

2 hours

TEST KITCHEN NOTES

THE COLOR OF THIS SIMPLE CONSOMMÉ WILL BE PALER THAN THAT OF COMMERCIAL CONSOMMÉ BUT THE FLAVOR, LACKING CHEMICAL ENHANCEMENTS AND PRESERVATIVES, WILL BE INFINITELY SUPERIOR. BECAUSE OF THE TIME REQUIRED, IT IS A GOOD IDEA TO MAKE CONSOMMÉ IN LARGE QUANTITY; WHAT YOU DON'T USE IMMEDIATELY WILL KEEP WELL IN THE FREEZER. SIMILARLY, THE COOKED MEAT MAY BE FROZEN AND PORTIONED OUT TO GARNISH SUBSEQUENT SOUPS OR STEWS.

BE VERY SPARING WITH SEASONINGS: 1 TEASPOON OF SALT IS PROBABLY ENOUGH; MORE MAY BE ADDED AT THE VERY END IF NECESSARY.

BEEF STOCK

YIELD: 10 CUPS (2.5L)

INGREDIENTS

2 pounds (1kg) lean beef,
    cut in small cubes
1 pound (500g) shin bone (with marrow),
    tied up in cheesecloth
3 quarts (3L) cold water
1 carrot, peeled
1 turnip, peeled
1 stalk celery
1 onion, unpeeled, stuck with 2 cloves
1 medium leek
1 clove garlic
1 sprig thyme
½ bay leaf
2 teaspoons kosher or sea salt
½ teaspoon peppercorns

1. Soak the beef and bone in the cold water for 30 minutes. At the end of that time, bring slowly to a simmer, reduce the heat and simmer for 1 hour.

2. Add the vegetables. Return to a simmer and cook gently for 3 to 4 hours, partially covered.

3. At the end of the cooking period, remove the meat, bone, and vegetables. Line a strainer or colander with a muslin cloth or several layers of dampened, wrung-out cheesecloth and strain the stock through it.

4. If you wish to reduce the stock before storing it, return it to the pot after straining and boil, uncovered, until reduced by half. Reducing the stock makes good sense because it will be used primarily as a recipe ingredient rather than as a soup on its own; make sure to mark containers of concentrated stock as you may want to dilute it with equal parts water when you use it.

Do not salt until you finish reducing, if at all. Store in the freezer in 1-cup (250ml) containers.

STANDING TIME

30 minutes

COOKING TIME

4 to 5½ hours

REDUCTION TIME

45 minutes

TEST KITCHEN NOTES

THE BROTH OBTAINED FROM THIS RECIPE WILL BE LIGHT IN COLOR. BE SURE TO LEAVE THE ONION UNPEELED; ITS SKIN WILL LEND COLOR TO THE STOCK. A DARKER VERSION WILL RESULT FROM BROWNING THE MEAT IN A 350°F (180°C) OVEN BEFORE SIMMERING. ONCE THE BROTH IS STRAINED IT WILL BE CLEAR ENOUGH FOR MOST DAY-TO-DAY USES; IF THE SPARKLING VERSION IS DESIRED, SEE PAGE 124 FOR DIRECTIONS FOR CLARIFYING STOCK.

THE MEAT AND VEGETABLES THUS COOKED FOR HOURS WILL NOT HAVE MUCH LEFT TO RECOMMEND THEM AND MAY BE DISCARDED. HOWEVER, IF YOU ARE THRIFTY, YOU MAY PURÉE THE VEGETABLES AND STORE THEM IN THE FREEZER TO THICKEN FUTURE VEGETABLE SOUPS, AND THE MEAT MAY BE USED TO EXTEND ANOTHER STEWED BEEF DISH IF THE SAUCE IS COPIOUS AND HIGHLY SPICED ENOUGH. IT WILL NOT CONTRIBUTE MUCH IN FLAVOR, HOWEVER.

THIS SEEMS LIKE A LOT OF COOKING FOR 2½ QUARTS (2.5L) OF STOCK (UNLESS YOU HAVE A REAL NEED TO CONTROL SALT INTAKE IN YOUR FAMILY, IN WHICH CASE IT MAKES PERFECT SENSE). THERE ARE EXCELLENT BEEF STOCKS AND CONSOMMÉS ON THE MARKET THAT MAY BE PERSONALIZED TO YOUR TASTE BY DIFFERENT MEANS. THEY MAY ALSO BE DILUTED AND USED AS STOCKS FOR THE FOUNDATION OF OTHER SOUPS.

BEEF CONSOMMÉ

INGREDIENTS

FOR THE STOCK

2½ pounds (1.25kg) lean beef,
    cut in small cubes
2¼ pounds (1.13kg) beef shin or ribs,
    or a combination
4 quarts (4L) cold water
1 teaspoon sea salt or kosher salt
1 pound (500g) carrots, peeled
½ pound (250g) turnips, peeled
½ pound (250g) leeks,
    trimmed and tied together
2 stalks celery with leaves
1 onion, unpeeled, stuck with 2 cloves
1 clove garlic, peeled
1 small sprig thyme
¼ bay leaf

FOR THE CONSOMMÉ

1 medium leek, white part only
1 medium carrot, peeled
1½ pounds (750g) lean beef,
    cut in small cubes
1 egg white, slightly beaten
3 quarts (3L) of beef stock

1. Make the stock: Crack any large bones; then tie the meat together with string. Place all the meat and bones in a stock pot with the water and bring to a boil, skimming off any foam that rises. Add the salt.

2. Put all the remaining ingredients into the stock pot, reduce the heat and barely simmer for 5 hours.

3. Let cool about 30 minutes, then degrease and strain through a cloth, dampened and wrung out, or through a fine strainer. You should have roughly 3 to 3½ quarts (3–3.5L).

4. Make the consommé: Rinse the leek carefully to eliminate grit. Chop the leek and carrot both fairly fine.

5. Stir the vegetables and meat together in a kettle with the egg white. Add the cooled beef stock and bring to a boil while stirring constantly. Reduce the heat until the pot is barely simmering. If the simmer is still too energetic, pull the pot partially off the burner. Cook, uncovered, over very low heat for 1½ hours.

6. At the end of the cooking time, degrease the consommé once more, and again strain it through a damp cloth. It should be quite clear, but you may if you wish clarify it (see page 124 for directions). Store in the freezer in 1-cup (250ml) containers.

COOKING TIME
FOR THE STOCK

5 hours

COOLING TIME
FOR THE STOCK

30 minutes

COOKING TIME
FOR THE CONSOMMÉ

1½ hours

TEST KITCHEN NOTES

IN SPITE OF THE TIME INVOLVED IN MAKING BEEF CONSOMMÉ, THIS IS NOT A DIFFICULT RECIPE. IT MAY BE COMPLETED IN ONE LONG DAY, OR IN TWO INSTALLMENTS. THE SECOND PORTION OF THE COOKING USES THE BROTH OF THE FIRST PART, AND BASICALLY DOUBLES THE FLAVOR. THE COLOR WILL BE PALER THAN THAT OF COMMERCIAL CONSOMMÉ AND THE FLAVOR, LACKING CHEMICAL ENHANCEMENTS AND PRESERVATIVES, INFINITELY SUPERIOR. IN VIEW OF THE TIME REQUIRED, IT SEEMS REASONABLE TO MAKE CONSOMMÉ IN LARGE QUANTITY; ANY EXTRA WILL KEEP WELL IN THE FREEZER. SIMILARLY, THE COOKED MEAT MAY BE FROZEN AND PORTIONED OUT TO GARNISH SUBSEQUENT SOUPS OR STEWS.

BE VERY SPARING WITH SEASONINGS: ¼ BAY LEAF REALLY IS ENOUGH, AND 1 TEASPOON OF SALT IS A GOOD START. MORE MAY BE ADDED AT THE VERY END IF NECESSARY.

VEGETABLE STOCK

INGREDIENTS

2 tablespoons (30ml) olive oil
    or vegetable oil
3 stalks celery, sliced fine
1 medium onion, sliced fine
2 quarts (2L) cold water
2 small turnips, peeled and diced
3 carrots, peeled and sliced fine
1 tomato, sliced
A few outer leaves of lettuce or
    cabbage, torn up
Bouquet garni (a sprig of thyme,
    a few stems of parsley, 1 bay leaf)
2 teaspoons salt
Freshly ground pepper

1. Heat the oil in a heavy stock pot over medium-high heat. Add the celery and onion and sauté until lightly browned, about 10 minutes.

2. Add the cold water, the rest of the vegetables, the bouquet garni, salt, and pepper. Bring slowly to a boil, reduce the heat and simmer for $1^{1}/_{2}$ hours.

3. Cool about 30 minutes, then strain. After straining, the vegetables may be puréed and used as thickening in other vegetable soups. There will be little if any degreasing of the stock necessary. Store in the refrigerator for several days or in 1-cup (250ml) containers in the freezer for several months.

COOKING TIME

1½ to 2 hours

COOLING TIME

30 minutes

TEST KITCHEN NOTES

USE VEGETABLES TO YOUR TASTE, BUT BE WARY OF DARK LEAVES THAT MAY BE BITTER, VEGETABLES WITH TOO PRONOUNCED A SWEETNESS, OR OF VEGETABLES THAT PRODUCE A COLOR THAT MAY NOT BE ACCEPTABLE FOR YOUR PURPOSES, SUCH AS BEETS. THE COOKING WATER FROM MANY DINNER VEGETABLES MAY ALSO BE USED AS PART OF THE STOCK. VEGETABLES THAT HAVE BEEN SITTING IN YOUR CRISPER FOR TOO LONG OFTEN HAVE STRONG FLAVOR AND MAY BE USED—IN STOCK, THEIR AGE MAY BE AN ASSET.

FISH FUMET

INGREDIENTS

1 small onion, sliced thin

1 stalk celery, with leaves

6 to 8 parsley stems, without leaves

1 small bay leaf

1 sprig thyme

¼ teaspoon peppercorns

2 to 3 pounds (1–1.5kg) fish heads, bones, and skins, including crab, lobster, and shrimp shells

1 cup (250ml) white wine

7 cups (1.75L) cold water

1 tablespoon (15ml) lemon juice

1 tablespoon (10g) salt

1. Place the onion in the stock pot with the celery, parsley stems, bay leaf, thyme, and peppercorns.

2. Rinse the fish parts, remove and discard the gills, and place the fish in the stock pot on top of the vegetables and seasonings. Add the wine, water, lemon juice, and salt. Bring slowly to a simmer. Skim if necessary. Simmer gently for 30 minutes. Strain through a colander, then a second time through a muslin cloth or a double layer of cheesecloth.

COOKING TIME

45 to 60 minutes

TEST KITCHEN NOTES

YOU MAY, IF YOU WISH, ADD UP TO 1 CUP (250ML) OF CLAM JUICE AND/OR OYSTER LIQUOR AT THE END OF COOKING. THIS WILL INTENSIFY THE FLAVOR AND EXTEND YOUR YIELD.

FUMET MAY BE CLARIFIED IF YOU THINK IT NECESSARY. USE AS SOON AS POSSIBLE AFTER COOKING; THE FLAVOR TENDS TO DETERIORATE RAPIDLY IN THE REFRIGERATOR. MAY BE STORED BRIEFLY IN THE FREEZER, BUT DO NOT MAKE IN ADVANCE JUST TO STORE. THIS IS A VERY TASTY, EASY, AND RELATIVELY QUICK STOCK TO MAKE.

IF THE FISH PARTS INCLUDED MORE THAN A CUP OR SO OF MEAT, PICK IT OUT OF THE STRAINER AND USE IN FISH CAKES. IT WILL NOT HAVE BEEN COOKED LONG ENOUGH TO LOSE ITS FLAVOR; INDEED, THE FLAVOR WILL HAVE BEEN ENHANCED BY THE OTHER INGREDIENTS.

LUNCHTIME SOUPS

Uncle Bill's Sausage Soup • Deb's Tortellini Soup • White Chili • Corn Chowder
Amish Succotash Chowder • Minestrone • Bilibi (Cold Mussel Soup)
Hearty Vegetable Beef Soup• Pistou • Spinach Soup with Rice• Potato Lentil Soup
Russian Cholodnik (Cucumber-Shrimp Soup) • Len's New Blue Cheese Soup
Cheese Soup • Amish Chilly Day Soup • French Onion Soup • Garlic Soup

DINNER SOUPS

Peanut Chicken Soup • Chicken and Oyster Soup • Scottish Hotch Potch
Cock-a-Leekie • Carbonnade à la Flamande (Flemish Beef Soup) • Gulyas (Goulash) Soup
Pot-au-Feu • Oxtail Soup • Mulligatawny Soup • Dutch Split Pea Soup
Pea Soup with Shrimp • Peanut, Pork, and Eggplant Soup
Zuppa di Ceci Avantagiatta (Quick Chick Pea Soup) • Turkey Soup with Dumplings
Brunswick Stew • Smoked Salmon Soup • New England Clam Chowder
Aran Scallop Soup • Manhattan Clam Chowder • Cajun Oyster Chowder
Chicken Gumbo • Smoky Corn Chowder • Oyster Stew • Seafood Gumbo
Domino Soup • Russian Shchi (Cabbage Soup) • Bouillabaisse • Ukrainian Borsch
Curaçao Coconut Soup • Thai Chicken Soup

PART TWO

MAIN COURSE SOUPS

LUNCHTIME SOUPS

There are no hard and fast rules dividing luncheon soups from dinner soups. There are, however, a few factors to consider. The degree of complexity of a given recipe is an important consideration—a recipe that requires three hours of careful attention is impractical for lunch. Another factor is the "weight" of the recipe—a light soup is better adapted to the noon meal than a heavy soup bordering on a stew. A related concern is the ingredients of the dish: many people tend not to eat their "meat meal" at noon, except on special occasions and Sundays, when the order is reversed.

In building a luncheon menu around a soup, keep in mind the nutritional building blocks: carbohydrates, proteins, vitamins, minerals, and so on. But plan with an eye to color and texture, too. Add a green salad for crunch, a Greek salad for color and crunch, bruschetta with tomato topping for starch and color, a platter of vegetable hors d'oeuvres to complement a meat- or fish-based soup, a plate of cold cuts to balance a vegetable soup. Even an appetizer soup can be the centerpiece of a satisfying lunch when accompanied by a sandwich made up of complementary ingredients.

For lunch, think in slightly smaller quantities than for dinner, but look for variety and don't restrict your imagination, which is a prime ingredient in any culinary effort.

UNCLE BILL'S SAUSAGE SOUP

SERVES 6

INGREDIENTS

5 leeks, white parts only

3 tablespoons (45g) butter

¾ pound (375g) lean smoked sausage

2 teaspoons ground cumin

2 medium potatoes, peeled and
    diced fine

4 cups (1L) Chicken Stock II (page 16)

Salt and freshly ground black pepper

½ cup (125ml) heavy cream

4 scallion greens (or chives), chopped
    fine

1. Slice the leeks in half lengthwise, rinse carefully, and pat dry. Slice cross-wise fairly thin. Melt the butter in a large saucepan over medium heat. Gently sauté the leeks in the butter until soft but not browned, about 10 minutes.

2. Cut the sausage in quarters length-wise, then cut in ¼-inch (8mm) slices. Add the sausage to the leeks with the ground cumin. Sauté for 5 to 6 minutes.

3. Add the potatoes to the saucepan with the chicken stock. Bring to a sim-mer and cook until the potatoes are done, 10 to 15 minutes. Add salt and pepper to taste.

4. Remove from the heat for a few minutes, then add the heavy cream and the scallion greens. Return to the heat to simmer for 5 minutes.

COOKING TIME

45 minutes

> ### TEST KITCHEN NOTES
>
> MY UNCLE BILL LIKES TO SERVE THIS SIMPLE, HEARTY SOUP AFTER A DAY ON THE SKI SLOPES. IT'S AN ADMIRABLE FILLER FOR A RAVENOUS CROWD COMING IN FROM THE COLD MUCH TOO EARLY FOR DINNER.

DEB'S TORTELLINI SOUP

INGREDIENTS

2 tablespoons (30ml) olive oil

1 medium onion, chopped

4 cloves garlic, minced

2 cups (425g) fresh chopped or canned
  crushed tomatoes

4 cups (1L) Chicken Stock II (page 16)

Pinch cayenne

2 cups (500g) fresh or frozen cheese
  tortellini

1 tablespoon (15g) butter

15 to 20 sorrel leaves

Salt and freshly ground black pepper,
  to taste

Grated Parmesan, for garnish

1. Heat the oil in a large saucepan over medium-high heat. Add the onion and garlic and sauté, stirring frequently, for 5 minutes.

2. Add the tomatoes to the onion mixture. Cook and stir for a few moments, then cover and cook over low heat, stirring occasionally, until the onions are transparent and the tomatoes disintegrate, 10 minutes at most.

3. Add the chicken stock and cayenne. Bring to a boil and add the tortellini. Return to a boil and cook until the pasta is tender, about 12 to 15 minutes.

4. While the pasta is cooking, rinse the sorrel and pat it dry. Tear off the stems, then slice the leaves horizontally in thin strips. Heat the butter in a small saucepan over medium-high heat. Quickly wilt the sorrel leaves in the butter, about 1 minute. When the pasta is cooked, stir the sorrel into the soup. Adjust the seasoning with salt and pepper.

5. Serve the soup, garnished with the Parmesan.

COOKING TIME

30 minutes

TEST KITCHEN NOTES

A HEARTY LUNCHEON SOUP WHEN ACCOMPANIED BY BREAD AND CHEESE, MY FRIEND DEB'S RECIPE CAN BE EASILY TRANSFORMED INTO A TASTY VEGETARIAN SOUP BY SUBSTITUTING VEGETABLE BROTH FOR THE CHICKEN.

THE FLAVOR IS QUITE ACIDIC; TO TAME THE ACIDITY, SUBSTITUTE A 10-OUNCE (300G) PACKAGE OF THAWED AND THOROUGHLY DRAINED, FROZEN CHOPPED SPINACH FOR THE SORREL LEAVES.

WHITE CHILI

INGREDIENTS

1 pound (500g) dried great Northern
    or any other small white beans

¼ cup (60ml) olive oil

2 medium onions, chopped

3 cloves garlic, minced very fine

2 green peppers, cored, seeded,
    and chopped

2 stalks celery

2 teaspoons dried oregano

2 teaspoons ground cumin

½ to 1 teaspoon cayenne

2 pounds (1kg) boned, skinless
    chicken breasts, diced into
    ½-inch (13mm) pieces

2 cups (500ml) Chicken Stock II
    (page 16)

2 cups (500ml) water

Salt and ground white pepper, to taste

1. Soak the beans in plenty of cold water overnight. If you missed this opportunity, there is a quicker method: cover the beans with cold water, bring them to a boil for 2 minutes, cover, and let stand for 1 hour off the heat. In either case, drain thoroughly, cover with fresh water, bring to a boil and simmer for 20 minutes. Drain and discard the cooking water.

2. Heat 2 tablespoons (30ml) olive oil in a large saucepan over medium-high heat. Add the onions, garlic, green peppers, and celery and sauté until the onions are translucent, about 10 minutes. Set aside.

3. While the vegetables are cooking, pound the oregano, cumin, and cayenne together in a mortar, or give them a spin in the blender. Stir these spices into the cooked vegetables.

4. Heat the remaining olive oil in a medium saucepan over medium heat. Add the chicken and quickly brown, about 5 minutes. Add to the cooked vegetables, beans, and the chicken stock and water. Simmer until the beans and chicken are just tender, 5 to 10 minutes.

5. Adjust the seasoning with salt and pepper and serve piping hot.

SOAKING TIME

overnight or at least 1 hour

COOKING TIME

40 minutes

TEST KITCHEN NOTES

BRUSCHETTA (PAGE 10) IS AN IDEAL ACCOMPANIMENT. THE PROPORTION OF MEAT TO BEANS AND THE ADDITION OF BRUSCHETTA AND, POSSIBLY, A MIXED GREEN SALAD MAKE THIS VERY PALE SOUP A TRUE MAIN DISH. MAKE A GOOD QUANTITY: THEY WILL ASK FOR SECONDS AND IT FREEZES WELL.

CORN CHOWDER

INGREDIENTS

2 ounces (60g) salt pork, diced

1 small onion, chopped fine

1 stalk celery, chopped fine

1 medium potato, peeled and diced

1 cup (250ml) water

½ bay leaf

Pinch cayenne

2 teaspoons flour

1½ cups (375ml) milk

1½ cups (270g) fresh corn kernels

¼ teaspoon salt (see Test Kitchen Notes)

1 tablespoon (10g) chopped cilantro

1. Sauté the salt pork in a large saucepan over medium-high heat until golden, about 10 minutes. Remove the pork bits from the pan, reserving them for garnish. Add the onion and celery to the pan; cook over medium-high heat until lightly browned, about 10 minutes.

2. Drain off the fat; add the potato, water, bay leaf, and cayenne to the vegetables. Bring to a boil, then simmer about 20 minutes, until the potatoes are tender.

3. Put the flour in a small bowl and blend in ½ cup (125ml) of the milk with a fork. Add this mixture to the pan, stirring until well blended. Simmer for 5 minutes to cook the flour.

4. In a small saucepan, simmer the corn in 1 cup (250ml) of milk for about 5 minutes, then add it to the chowder.

5. Adjust the seasoning with salt; you may add up to an extra ½ cup (125ml) milk if the chowder is too thick.

6. Serve piping hot, garnished with chopped cilantro and the reserved salt pork niblets.

COOKING TIME

50 to 55 minutes

TEST KITCHEN NOTES

TO THIS DAY I THINK BACK TO THE TIME WHEN I LONGED FOR THE GOLDEN BITS OF SALT PORK TO WHICH ONLY MY UNCLE WAS ENTITLED ON CHOWDER DAYS. I DON'T KNOW WHY THEY WERE EXCLUSIVELY HIS, BUT NO SUCH EXCLUSION GOES ON IN MY HOUSEHOLD, THOUGH I DO CONTINUE TO SERVE THEM SEPARATELY, CRISP AND TANTALIZING. OF COURSE, YOU CAN LEAVE THEM TO COOK WITH THE CHOWDER ITSELF, IF YOU LIKE. FOR A MORE ELEGANT APPEARANCE, YOU MAY WISH TO SAUTÉ THE VEGETABLES IN 2 TABLESPOONS OF BUTTER AT THE OUTSET, AND COOK THE SALT PORK GARNISH ENTIRELY APART. THE AMOUNT OF SALT YOU ADD WILL VARY GREATLY DEPENDING ON THE METHOD YOU CHOOSE.

AMISH SUCCOTASH CHOWDER

INGREDIENTS

4 tablespoons (60g) butter
1 medium onion, chopped
1 medium potato, peeled and diced
1 cup (250ml) water
1 cup (180g) lima beans
1 cup (180g) corn kernels
About 1 cup (250ml) heavy cream
2 tablespoons (20g) flour
2 cups (500ml) cold milk
Salt and freshly ground black pepper,
     to taste
Fresh parsley, chopped, for garnish

1. Melt 2 tablespoons (30g) butter in a large saucepan over medium-high heat. Sauté the onion until it begins to brown, about 10 minutes.

2. Add the potato and water. Cover and cook for 15 minutes or until tender.

3. If the lima beans are fresh, add them along with the potatoes; if frozen, add them with the corn for the last 5 minutes of the cooking of the potatoes.

4. When the vegetables are done, drain the cooking liquid and measure it; you should have about 1 cup (250 ml). Add an equal amount of heavy cream. Set the vegetables aside.

5. In the saucepan, make a béchamel sauce: Melt the remaining 2 tablespoons of butter, stir in the flour, then cook and stir for a moment over low heat to incorporate; gradually add the milk, stirring constantly. Cook for a few minutes, still stirring; return the vegetables, cooking liquid, and heavy cream to the saucepan and heat to a simmer. Add salt and pepper to taste.

6. Serve, garnished with chopped parsley.

COOKING TIME

30 minutes

TEST KITCHEN NOTES

AMISH COOKING IS VERY PLAIN (NOT FOR NOTHING ARE THEY CALLED "THE PLAIN PEOPLE") BUT IT IS HEARTY AND HEALTHY TO MATCH THEIR ACTIVE LIFESTYLE. THE TEMPTATION IS TO ADD SPICES, BUT AMISH SELF-SUFFICIENCY TENDS TO PRECLUDE THE MORE EXOTIC IMPORTED SPICES. YOU ARE, OF COURSE FREE TO ALTER, BUT THIS MEATLESS, UNADORNED RECIPE WITH ITS BUTTER AND CREAM IS OF SURPASSING DELICACY AND SURPRISING RICHNESS OF FLAVOR AS IT STANDS.

MINESTRONE

INGREDIENTS

½ cup (70g) dried red kidney beans

3 tablespoons (45ml) olive oil

1 medium onion, chopped

2 or 3 cloves garlic, minced

¼ pound (125g) cabbage leaves,
    chopped (no core)

1 medium potato, peeled and diced

1 large carrot, peeled and diced

3 celery stalks with leaves, diced

1 small zucchini, diced

½ pound (250g) green beans,
    cut in ¾-inch (2cm) lengths

1 pound (500g) fresh chopped or
    canned crushed tomatoes

8 cups (2L) Chicken Stock II (page 16) or
    Vegetable Stock (page 20)

½ cup (60g) small pasta

½ cup (90g) peas, optional

Salt and freshly ground black pepper

Grated Parmesan or Romano cheese,
    for garnish

1. Soak the kidney beans overnight in cold water. Or for a quicker method, put them in a saucepan with plenty of water, bring gently to a boil, and simmer for 2 minutes. Remove from the heat, cover tightly, and let stand for 1 hour. Whichever method you use, drain the beans before cooking. Place the beans in a saucepan with cold water to cover generously, bring to a simmer, and cook until tender, 45 to 60 minutes.

2. While the beans are cooking, heat the olive oil in a saucepan over medium heat. Add the onion and garlic and gently sauté until tender but not browned, about 10 minutes.

3. While the beans are cooking, add the cabbage, potato, carrot, celery, zucchini, and green beans. For the best results, all the vegetables should be relatively the same size. Cook, stirring frequently, for 2 to 3 minutes.

4. Stir the tomatoes into the vegetables with the stock; bring to a simmer and cook 30 minutes or until the vegetables are tender.

5. When the vegetables are almost tender, add the cooked kidney beans, the pasta, and the peas, if you are using them. Cook until the pasta is al dente, not mushy, about 10 minutes. Adjust the seasoning with salt and pepper.

6. Serve piping hot with grated Parmesan, and perhaps some Garlic Bread (page 11) on the side.

SOAKING TIME

overnight or at least 1 hour

COOKING TIME

about 1 hour

TEST KITCHEN NOTES

SOAKING THE BEANS OVERNIGHT IS A GENTLER METHOD OF REHYDRATING THEM, AND YOU STAND A BETTER CHANCE OF KEEPING THEM INTACT THROUGH THE COOKING PROCESS, ALTHOUGH THERE IS NOTHING WRONG WITH THE QUICKER METHOD.

MINESTRONE MEANS "BIG SOUP," AND THERE ARE PROBABLY AS MANY VERSIONS OF THIS SOUP AS THERE ARE ITALIANS WHO COOK, SO FEEL FREE TO IMPROVISE. CLASSIC MILANESE MINESTRONE USES CHOPPED SPINACH (2 CUPS [500G]) INSTEAD OF GREEN BEANS, SAGE AND RICE INSTEAD OF BEANS AND POTATO. "PLAIN" MINESTRONE IS MADE WITH WATER INSTEAD OF BROTH. WHITE BEANS AND/OR CHICK PEAS MAY BE SUBSTITUTED FOR KIDNEY BEANS. YOU MAY LIKE TO USE, SPARINGLY, YOUR FAVORITE ITALIAN HERBS: PARSLEY, OREGANO, BASIL, FOR EXAMPLE.

BILIBI

(Cold Mussel Soup)

SERVES 6

INGREDIENTS

6 pounds (3kg) mussels, in their shells

1½ cups (375ml) dry white wine

2 shallots, minced

Bouquet garni (½ teaspoon dried or
    1 sprig each of parsley, tarragon,
    and thyme and ½ bay leaf)

Ground white pepper, to taste

4 cups (1L) Fish Fumet (page 21)

¾ cup (187.5ml) sour cream

¾ cup (187.5ml) milk

1 tablespoon (10g) chopped chives,
    for garnish

1. Rinse and scrub the mussels, discarding any that may be open. Put the white wine and shallots in a large saucepan with the bouquet garni and a little ground white pepper. Add the mussels, cover tightly, and cook over high heat for about 5 minutes to open the mussels as quickly as possible. Shake the pot occasionally to distribute the heat evenly.

2. Discard any mussels that do not open, then strain off and reserve the cooking liquid. Scoop the mussels out of their shells, discarding the latter and setting aside the meat.

3. Combine the fumet, the liquid from the mussels, the sour cream, and milk in a soup tureen. Refrigerate until ready to serve, about 2 hours. At that time, add the mussels to the soup and garnish with chopped chives.

COOKING TIME

45 minutes

CHILLING TIME

2 hours

TEST KITCHEN NOTES

THIS DELICIOUS SOUP WAS CREATED BY CHEF LOUIS BARTHE AT MAXIM'S IN PARIS FOR THE AMERICAN TIN TYCOON WILLIAM B. LEED. IT IS A WONDERFUL SUMMER DISH, ACCOMPANIED BY BRUSCHETTAS (PAGE 10) TOPPED WITH CHOPPED FRESH TOMATOES, AND A PLATTER OF CORN-ON-THE-COB.

HEARTY VEGETABLE BEEF SOUP

SERVES 6

INGREDIENTS

1 1-pound (500g) meaty soup bone
   (beef shin or shank)

½ cup (90g) chopped green pepper

1 small onion, chopped

1 small carrot, chopped

1 stalk celery, chopped

2 or 3 cloves garlic, minced

4 peppercorns

1 teaspoon salt

4 cups (1L) cold water

½ cup (90g) frozen or canned
   black-eyed peas

½ cup (90g) fresh diced green beans

½ cup (90g) frozen lima beans

2 cups (500ml) mixed vegetable juice

½ cup (90g) green peas

½ cup (90g) corn kernels

Pinch cayenne

1 tablespoon (15ml) Worcestershire
   sauce, optional

3 cups (750g) cooked macaroni

1. Place the soup bone in a large pot with the pepper, onion, carrot, celery, garlic, peppercorns, and salt. Add the cold water and bring very slowly to a boil. Reduce the heat and simmer for 2 hours or until the meat is tender.

2. Add the black-eyed peas to the pot after 1½ hours.

3. While the meat is cooking, cook the green beans and lima beans in the vegetable juice for 10 minutes. Add the peas and corn and simmer just long enough to heat them through. Remove the saucepan from the heat.

4. When the meat is tender, remove it from the broth. Remove any gristle and fat and dice the meat fairly fine. Return it to the pot, adding the vegetable mixture at the same time. Adjust the seasoning with salt and pepper, stirring in a pinch of cayenne and the Worcestershire sauce. Simmer for 5 minutes to blend the flavors.

5. Serve piping hot with a ½ cup (125g) scoop of macaroni in each bowl and an accompaniment of hot cornbread.

COOKING TIME

2 to 2½ hours

TEST KITCHEN NOTES

THIS RECIPE REPRESENTS THE ULTIMATE IN ADAPTABILITY. EXCEPT FOR THE FIRST GROUP OF VEGETABLES, WHICH MUST BE FRESH TO FLAVOR THE STOCK, THE REST OF THE VEGETABLES MAY BE FRESH, FROZEN, CANNED, MIXED OR SEPARATE, OR LEFT-OVER. THE BLACK-EYED PEAS MAY ALSO BE RECONSTITUTED, FROZEN, FRESH, OR CANNED (BE SURE TO RINSE THEM IF CANNED). IF YOU LACK ANY OF THE LATTER ELEMENTS, YOU CAN SUBSTITUTE OKRA, CAULIFLOWER, CHICK PEAS, TURNIPS, CABBAGE—THE POSSIBILITIES ARE AS NUMEROUS AS THE CONTENTS OF YOUR REFRIGERATOR AND PANTRY. IT IS A GREAT LUNCHEON SOUP—COMPLETE AND SATISFYING, BUT NOT HEAVY.

PISTOU

INGREDIENTS

FOR THE PISTOU

10-12 leaves fresh basil
(1 teaspoon dried)
2 leaves fresh sage (½ teaspoon dried)
2 or 3 sprigs thyme, leaves only
(½ teaspoon)
2 cloves garlic
1 tablespoon (15ml) tomato paste
2 tablespoons (30ml) extra-virgin
olive oil

FOR THE SOUP

10 haricots blancs beans, or ⅓ cup (60g)
frozen black-eyed peas
4 cups (1L) water
¼ pound (45g) green beans, diced
2 small potatoes, peeled and diced
2 plum tomatoes, peeled, seeded, and
diced (see Test Kitchen Notes)
½ cup (60g) broken vermicelli
Salt and freshly ground black pepper,
to taste
Grated Parmesan, for garnish

1. Make the Pistou: Place the basil, sage, and thyme in a mortar with the garlic and pound to a paste. Pound in the tomato paste, then gradually add the olive oil, pounding all the while. Alternatively, you may mince the garlic by hand, then toss all of these ingredients into the blender to make a thin paste. Set aside.

2. Make the soup: Pop the haricots blancs out of their parent beans (I used the seeds of tough, overgrown green beans).

3. In a large saucepan, bring the water to a boil. Add the green beans, haricots or black-eyed peas, potatoes, and tomatoes and then simmer until the potatoes are not quite tender, about 20 minutes.

3. Bring the soup back to a boil and toss in the vermicelli. Cook until al dente, about 10 minutes. Adjust the seasoning with salt and pepper.

5. To serve, place the Pistou in the bottom of a tureen and pour the hot soup over it. Garnish with the Parmesan.

COOKING TIME

45 minutes

TEST KITCHEN NOTES

THIS FAIRLY SIMPLE SOUP, SO REMINISCENT OF PESTO, IS WILDLY POPULAR IN SOUTHERN FRANCE, BUT WAS ACTUALLY ADOPTED FROM NORTHERN ITALY. THE FLAVORS OF GARLIC, BASIL, AND SAGE PREDOMINATE; SOME COOKS ADD TWO EGG YOLKS TO THE PISTOU MIXTURE, BUT I DON'T FIND THAT THEY ADD ANYTHING TO A SOUP WHOSE CHARM LIES IN ITS STRONG, STRAIGHTFOR-WARD EARTHINESS.

THE EASIEST WAY TO PEEL TOMATOES IS TO DUNK THEM IN BOILING WATER FOR A FEW SECONDS. WHEN THE SKINS BREAK, REMOVE THE TOMATOES WITH A SLOTTED SPOON AND RUN UNDER COLD WATER. WHEN THEY ARE COOL ENOUGH TO HANDLE, THE SKINS WILL SLIP OFF EASILY.

Spinach Soup with Rice

SERVES 6

INGREDIENTS

2 tablespoons (30ml) olive oil

1 medium onion, diced

1 stalk celery, diced

1 carrot, diced

2 medium tomatoes, chopped

2 cloves garlic, minced

1 cup (250g) chopped, cooked spinach
(1 10-ounce [300g] package,
thawed)

Pinch cayenne

4 cups (1L) Chicken Stock II (page 16)

Salt and freshly ground black pepper,
to taste

1 cup (150g) cooked rice

½ cup (60g) grated Parmesan cheese,
for garnish

1. Heat 1 tablespoon (15ml) olive oil in a large saucepan over medium heat. Add the onion, celery, and carrot and sauté until tender but not browned, about 10 minutes.

2. Add the tomatoes and garlic to the vegetables and cook together for about 5 minutes, adding the remaining oil as necessary.

3. While the tomatoes are cooking, press out all excess moisture from the spinach through a sieve. Add it to the tomato mixture with a generous pinch of cayenne.

4. Add the stock and bring to a simmer. Adjust the seasoning with salt and pepper. Just before serving, add the cooked rice and heat thoroughly. Serve, garnished with Parmesan cheese.

COOKING TIME

30 minutes

Potato Lentil Soup

SERVES 4

INGREDIENTS

1 cup (100g) dried brown lentils

¼ pound (125g) salt pork, diced

1 medium onion, diced

2 small potatoes, peeled and diced

1 stalk celery, diced

1 clove garlic, crushed

4 cups (1L) Beef Stock (page 18)

¼ teaspoon ground cumin

Pinch cayenne

½ green pepper, seeded and diced

Salt and freshly ground black pepper,
to taste

1. Pick over the lentils, rinse, cover with an inch or so of cold water, bring to a boil, and simmer for 20 minutes or until just tender but not mushy. Drain and set aside.

2. While the lentils are cooking, sauté the salt pork until golden in a large saucepan over medium-high heat, about 10 minutes. Strain off all but 3 tablespoons (45ml) of the fat, but do not discard. Set aside the pork bits.

3. Return the saucepan to the heat. Add the onion, potatoes, and celery and sauté for 5 minutes or so, until the onions are translucent. Add the garlic, stock, cumin, and cayenne. Bring to a boil, cover, and simmer for about 10 minutes or until the potatoes are tender. Add salt and pepper to taste.

4. To serve, add the lentils to the soup along with the green pepper and heat to a simmer. Serve hot, accompanied by the salt pork, handed around separately, and Bruschetta or Garlic Bread (pages 10 or 11).

COOKING TIME

About 45 minutes

RUSSIAN CHOLODNIK
(Cucumber-Shrimp Soup)

INGREDIENTS

½ pound (250g) medium shrimp

1 cup unpeeled, seeded, and diced
    cucumber

½ teaspoon ground fennel

1 clove garlic, pressed

1 tablespoon (15g) grated onion

1 teaspoon fresh dill, chopped

4 cups (1L) buttermilk

Salt and ground white pepper,
    to taste

1. Bring a pot of salted water to a boil. Add the shrimp and cook until just done, about 5 minutes, being careful not to overcook. Drain, peel, and dice shrimp, saving 4 whole (tails on), for garnish.

2. Stir all the ingredients together in a bowl and let stand at room temperature for 1 hour or so. Adjust the seasoning with salt and pepper. Chill thoroughly before serving, at least 1½ hours.

COOKING TIME

5 minutes

CHILLING TIME

1½ hours

TEST KITCHEN NOTES

TRADITIONALLY, THIS SOUP IS A POLISH DISH FEATURING BEETS, AND OCCASIONALLY VEAL, AND IS SPELLED "CHLODNIK." THIS VARIATION IS ADAPTED FROM A COOKBOOK WRITTEN IN FRENCH BY A RUSSIAN COOK IN 1934.

AS YOU WILL SEE, THE SIMPLE COMBINATION OF CUCUMBER AND SHRIMP MAKES THIS A SUBSTANTIAL SOUP. SERVE IT WITH FRESH FRUIT, BREAD, AND CHEESE FOR THE IDEAL SUMMER LUNCHEON.

LEN'S NEW BLUE CHEESE SOUP

SERVES 4

INGREDIENTS

3 tablespoons (45g) butter

1 shallot, minced fine

¼ cup (35g) flour

4 cups (1L) whole milk

1 cup (125g) crumbled blue cheese

1 teaspoon dried herbs: bouquet garni,
    herbes de Provence, or Italian herbs

½ cup (80g) cauliflower florets

½ cup (80g) broccoli florets

Salt and ground white pepper,
    to taste

Croutons toasted with olive oil
    (page 11), for garnish

1. Melt the butter in a heavy-bottomed saucepan over medium heat. Add the shallot and cook it slowly until translucent, about 10 minutes. Add the flour and cook for a few minutes over medium heat to incorporate. Gradually add the milk, stirring constantly. Bring to a simmer and cook, stirring frequently, for 5 minutes. Add the blue cheese and the herbs; continue to cook gently and stir until the cheese melts. Set aside.

2. Meanwhile, cook the cauliflower and broccoli florets in boiling water to blanch for 1 to 2 minutes. Rinse under cold water and drain thoroughly before adding to the soup.

3. Reheat the soup thoroughly but gently before serving; do not allow to boil. Adjust the seasoning with the salt and pepper. Serve immediately, garnished with the croutons.

COOKING TIME

25 minutes

TEST KITCHEN NOTES

THIS VERY SOPHISTICATED SOUP WAS CONTRIBUTED BY MY HUSBAND. FOR THE BEST RESULTS, USE THE HIGHEST-QUALITY BLUE CHEESE YOU CAN FIND.

CHEESE SOUP

INGREDIENTS

2 tablespoons (30g) butter

1 medium onion, minced

2 stalks celery, with leaves, minced

1 clove garlic, minced or crushed

4 medium potatoes, peeled and diced

4 cups (1L) Chicken Stock II (page 16)

¼ teaspoon ground cumin

1 cup (250ml) premium beer

2 cups (250g) grated sharp
   Cheddar cheese

1½ cups (188g) grated Swiss cheese

½ cup (125ml) heavy cream

½ teaspoon (2.25ml)
   Worcestershire sauce

Pinch cayenne

Salt and freshly ground black pepper

Paprika and chopped chives or scallion
   greens, for garnish

1. Melt the butter in a large saucepan over medium heat. Add the onion and celery and sauté until tender but not browned, about 10 minutes.

2. Add the garlic, potatoes, stock, and cumin to the saucepan. Bring to a simmer; cook until the potatoes are very soft, about 15 minutes. Roughly mash the potatoes in the saucepan, then put the soup through a food mill or whirl briefly in the blender in batches. The desired effect is not a very smooth purée but rather a rough one.

3. Return the soup to the saucepan, add the beer, and bring to a simmer. Add the Cheddar and Swiss cheese and cook gently, stirring constantly, until all the cheese is melted, about 5 minutes. Stir in the cream, Worcestershire sauce, and a tiny pinch of cayenne. Adjust the seasoning with salt and pepper. Reheat thoroughly but gently.

4. Serve, garnished with a sprinkling of paprika and chopped chives or scallions and chunks of crusty country bread or buttered toast for dunking.

COOKING TIME

45 minutes

AMISH CHILLY DAY SOUP

INGREDIENTS

2 medium onions, chopped fine

1 large potato, peeled and cubed

1 carrot, peeled and diced

1 stalk celery, chopped

1 tablespoon (15g) rice

1 tablespoon (15g) macaroni

3 cups (750ml) Chicken Stock I (page 15)

1 raw chicken breast or ½ pound (250g)
   cooked chicken, cubed

1 cup (250ml) heavy cream

Salt and ground white pepper, to taste

1. Place all the vegetables in a saucepan along with the rice and macaroni, and add the chicken stock. If you are using an uncooked chicken breast, add it now. Bring to a boil and simmer until the potato is tender, about 30 minutes.

2. Add precooked chicken now, if you are using it. Stir in the heavy cream and reheat gently but do not boil. Add salt and pepper to taste.

COOKING TIME

45 minutes

FRENCH ONION SOUP

INGREDIENTS

5 tablespoons (75g) butter

1 large onion, sliced fine

2 tablespoons (20g) flour

6 cups (1.5L) Chicken Consommé
  (page 17)

18 slices bread cut from a baguette,
  ¼- to ½-inch (6–12mm) thick

3 cups (375g) grated imported Swiss
  cheese, half Comté and half
  Emmenthal, if possible

1. Melt the butter in a heavy-bottomed saucepan. Add the onion and cook over very low heat for about 30 minutes, stirring frequently. The onion slices should not be browned, but uniformly and lightly golden, with no crisp edges.

2. Add the flour. Let it brown lightly, stirring constantly for about 5 minutes. Stir the consommé into the onions, gradually at first to avoid lumps. Bring to a boil and let simmer for 30 minutes.

3. While the soup is simmering, toast the bread; place three slices in the bottom of each bowl; sprinkle ⅓ cup (40g) of the grated cheese evenly over the toast in each bowl, setting aside the remainder for topping.

4. Preheat the broiler, or preheat the oven to 425°F (220°C). Pour the soup gently over the cheese and toast. The bread will float to the top. Sprinkle the remaining cheese over each portion. Brown under the broiler for 5 minutes or so, or heat in the oven until the cheese is browned, about 10 minutes. Serve in the cooking vessels.

COOKING TIME

1¼ hours

TEST KITCHEN NOTES

THIS IS THE QUINTESSENTIAL FRENCH SOUP. IT IS USUALLY FINISHED AND SERVED IN TERRA COTTA MINI-TUREENS, AS SERVING THE ROPY MELTED SWISS CHEESE FROM A LARGE TUREEN IS NEARLY IMPOSSIBLE. IF YOU DO NOT HAVE ACCESS TO A VARIETY OF SWISS CHEESES, USE WHAT YOU CAN FIND, BUT TRY TO GET THE IMPORTED VARIETY FOR ITS INIMITABLE NUTTY FLAVOR. SOME COOKS ADD WINE AS A FINISHING TOUCH, BUT TO MY MIND THIS REFINEMENT ONLY SERVES TO CONFUSE THE PALATE. SIMPLE AS IT IS, ONION SOUP IS A MEAL IN ITSELF, PERFECTLY COMPLEMENTED BY A ROBUST SALAD.

DO NOT USE SWEET ONIONS IN THIS RECIPE; THE ORDINARY YELLOW VARIETY IS MORE SAVORY TO COOK WITH.

GARLIC SOUP

SERVES 4

INGREDIENTS

20 cloves garlic

2 tablespoons (30ml) olive oil

4 teaspoons flour

5 cups (1.25L) water

Salt and freshly ground black pepper,
      to taste

1 ounce (30g) vermicelli,
      broken in ½-inch (13mm) pieces

1 egg, separated

1 teaspoon (5ml) wine vinegar

1. Peel the garlic cloves without crushing. Warm the olive oil in a saucepan, add the garlic, and cook gently for a few minutes. To avoid any bitterness the garlic must not brown. It should be barely golden.

2. Stir in the flour and cook 2 to 3 minutes longer, then gradually add the water, stirring constantly to avoid lumps. Add a pinch of salt and a little pepper, cover, and let simmer 20 to 30 minutes over low heat.

3. Add the vermicelli and let cook 8 minutes.

4. Slip the egg white into the soup, allowing it to poach for 2 or 3 minutes; using a slotted spoon or skimmer, remove the poached white and place it in the bottom of a tureen.

5. Using a fork, lightly beat the vinegar into the yolk in a small bowl. Stirring constantly, drizzle ¼ cup (125ml) of the hot soup into the egg yolk and vinegar mixture, then return the whole to the saucepan. Over low heat, return the soup to a simmer for a moment to bind the soup. Adjust the seasoning with salt if necessary and a grating of fresh pepper. Pour the soup into the tureen over the poached egg white and serve immediately.

COOKING TIME

About 1 hour

TEST KITCHEN NOTES

THE ONLY STARTLING THING ABOUT THIS RECIPE IS THE NUMBER OF GARLIC CLOVES IN IT; THE FLAVOR IS DELECTABLE, THE TEXTURE SILKY. THE PUNGENCY OF THE GARLIC FLAVOR IS COOKED INTO DELICIOUS SUBMISSION, DESPITE THE PRESENCE OF THE WHOLE GARLIC CLOVES. KEEP IN MIND THAT THE PASTA WILL CONTINUE TO ABSORB LIQUID AND THUS THICKEN THE SOUP, SO THAT ONLY THE FIRST TWO STEPS CAN BE PREPARED IN ADVANCE.

DINNER SOUPS

In general, the soups in this chapter differ from luncheon soups in three ways: first, they may be more complex either in the number or nature of their ingredients; second, their preparation may be longer and more intricate; and third, each one includes a full complement of animal and/or vegetable protein. Some also include all of the vegetables necessary to complete the meal, although you may still wish to serve the accompaniments suggested with specific recipes, such as cream cheese tartlets, corn on the cob in season, garlic bread, rolls and butter, or a salad. An excellent finish for a soup-centered meal, often a rich and hearty experience in itself, is fruit, in a salad, on a shortcake, in a pie, or raw and whole. In all things, consider the balance of the foods being consumed, their colors and their textures. Much of cooking depends upon common sense, the true sixth sense.

PEANUT CHICKEN SOUP

SERVES 6

INGREDIENTS

3 tablespoons (45ml) peanut, corn,
    or olive oil
1 4-pound (2kg) chicken, cut up in six
    pieces (or 5 or 6 chicken breasts,
    cut into bite-size pieces)
1 medium onion, chopped
1 large tomato, chopped, or 1 cup
    (240g) canned crushed tomatoes
2 or 3 tablespoons (30 or 45ml)
    tomato paste
½ teaspoon salt
¼ teaspoon cayenne
2 bay leaves
Bouquet garni (parsley, thyme, sage)
1 cup (250g) natural peanut butter
    or ground peanuts
2 cups (500ml) water
6 medium potatoes, peeled and boiled,
    then cubed
¼ pound (125g) small shrimp, peeled
    and deveined

1. Heat the oil in a large saucepan over medium-high heat. Sauté the chicken and onion in the oil until browned, about 15 minutes.

2. Add the tomato, tomato paste, salt, cayenne, bay leaves, and bouquet garni to the chicken, stirring until well blended. Cover and cook, stirring occasionally, about 20 minutes, until the chicken is cooked through.

3. Add the peanut butter and water, stirring until well blended. Cover and cook over low heat for another 20 minutes or so.

4. When the soup is done, add the shrimp and potatoes, cooking gently for the few minutes necessary to cook the shrimp. Adjust the seasoning; add water if the soup is too thick.

COOKING TIME

1 hour

TEST KITCHEN NOTES

THIS IS NOT A COMPLEX SOUP, BUT IT IS A VERY HEARTY ONE, PERHAPS BEST SERVED IN COOL WEATHER. THE ORIGINAL RECIPE IS FIERY INDEED, BUT THIS IS A GENTLER VERSION. ADD AS MUCH CAYENNE AS YOU CAN BEAR, BUT REMEMBER THAT CAYENNE TENDS TO DEVELOP AS IT COOKS AND IT MAY SURPRISE YOU IN THE END.

CHICKEN AND OYSTER SOUP

INGREDIENTS

1 cup (250ml) dry white wine

1 pound (500g) oysters, shucked, their
    liquor reserved

4 cups (1L) Chicken Stock I (page 15)

½ cup (90g) green peas, fresh or frozen

1 carrot, diced fine

3 tablespoons (45g) butter

1 shallot, minced

2 tablespoons (20g) parsley, minced

1 sprig fresh tarragon, chopped,
    or ½ teaspoon dried

½ pound (250g) mushrooms, sliced fine

2 tablespoons (20g) flour

1½ cups (180g) cooked diced chicken

Salt and ground white pepper, to taste

Pinch cayenne

½ cup (125ml) heavy cream

Juice of ½ lemon

1. Bring the wine to a simmer and plunge in the oysters. Simmer for 2 minutes and drain, reserving the liquid.

2. In a saucepan, combine the oyster liquor, the wine used to poach the oysters, and the chicken stock. Bring to a boil, then add the peas and diced carrot and simmer until just tender, about 5 to 10 minutes.

3. Meanwhile, heat the butter in a large saucepan over medium-high heat. Sauté the shallot, parsley, tarragon, and mushrooms in the butter until the mushrooms are just done, that is, before they "juice up," about 10 minutes. Sprinkle with flour, then dilute with a little of the chicken stock mixture.

4. Add the remaining stock mixture to the mushroom mixture, then stir in the diced chicken, salt, white pepper, cayenne, and heavy cream.

5. Bring the soup to a simmer and add the oysters and lemon juice at the very last minute before serving, warming thoroughly without boiling.

COOKING TIME

30 minutes

TEST KITCHEN NOTES

IN COLONIAL AMERICA, OYSTERS WERE PLENTIFUL IN NEW ENGLAND AND CHICKEN WAS NOT, SO A CHICKEN PIE WAS LIKELY TO BE "EXTENDED" BY THE ADDITION OF OYSTERS AS A FILLER. ALTHOUGH THE TABLES HAVE TURNED TODAY, THIS SOUP IS WELCOME AS A MAIN DISH WITH ITS ELEGANT TWIST ON THE CLASSIC CHICKEN POT PIE. YOU MAY WISH TO ACCOMPANY THIS SOUP WITH BITE-SIZED LOZENGES OR ROUNDS OF FLAKY PIE CRUST, BAKED FOR THE OCCASION AND HANDED AROUND SEPARATELY TO BE FLOATED ON THE SOUP.

IF YOU DO NOT HAVE COOKED CHICKEN ON HAND, USE A CHICKEN BREAST, DICED, AND SIMMER IT IN THE CHICKEN STOCK WITH THE PEAS AND DICED CARROTS.

SCOTTISH HOTCH POTCH

SERVES 6 TO 8

INGREDIENTS

2 pounds (1kg) neck of lamb
2 quarts (2L) cold water
2 teaspoons salt
Freshly ground pepper, to taste
Bouquet garni (parsley, rosemary,
    celery leaves)
1 carrot, diced fine
1 small turnip, diced fine
½ pound (250g) cauliflower,
    cut into small florets
½ pound (250g) green beans, diced
1 small head of Bibb lettuce, leaves cut
    horizontally into thin slices
1 cup (180g) green peas, fresh or frozen
Chopped parsley, for garnish

1. Remove any excess fat from the neck (or "scrag" bones as they are called in Scotland). Place the bones in the cold water and bring to a simmer very slowly.

2. Add the bouquet garni. Cover and simmer for 30 minutes.

3. Add the carrot and turnip to the soup, then cover the pot again and continue to simmer for another 1½ hours.

4. Add the green beans, lettuce, and peas, and cook for an additional 30 minutes.

5. Remove the bones and bouquet garni from the soup, cool enough to handle, and remove the meat from the bones. Cut into bite-size pieces and return the meat to the soup. Adjust the seasoning with salt and pepper.

6. Garnish with the parsley. A few potatoes served on the side will make a complete meal of this soup.

COOKING TIME

2½ to 3 hours

TEST KITCHEN NOTES

SHEEP HAVE BEEN DOMESTICATED FOR THOUSANDS OF YEARS, SO IT IS HARDLY SURPRISING THAT LAMB CONTINUES TO FIGURE PROMINENTLY IN MANY WORLD CUISINES, INCLUDING THOSE OF THE BRITISH ISLES.

BECAUSE I AM NOT A BIG FAN OF COLD LAMB SANDWICHES, I AM ALWAYS ON THE LOOKOUT FOR USES FOR LEFTOVER LAMB. THIS IS A GOOD ONE, AS LONG AS THE COOKED LAMB IS SUPPLEMENTED BY A LITTLE FRESH MEAT TO FLAVOR THE STOCK.

COCK-A-LEEKIE

INGREDIENTS

12 pitted prunes
1 3½-pound (1.75kg) stewing hen or
    chicken, the tougher the better,
    giblets included
1 pound (500g) leeks
Bouquet garni (thyme, bay leaf,
    rosemary, parsley)
6 white peppercorns
2 teaspoons sea or kosher salt
4 tablespoons (40g) cornstarch, optional
4 tablespoons (60ml) water, optional
Chopped parsley, for garnish

1. Soak the prunes overnight in cold water to cover.

2. Rinse the chicken. Place it in a pot with its giblets and water to cover, and bring very slowly to a simmer.

3. Wash and trim the leeks. Slice the white portions in rounds, discarding the greens. When the soup is simmering, add the leeks to it, along with the bouquet garni, peppercorns, and salt.

4. Continue to cook the chicken at a simmer until tender, about 1½ hours.

5. When tender, remove the chicken from the pot. Drain the prunes and add to the broth to cook for 20 minutes while you skin and bone the chicken. Cut the meat and giblets in bite-size pieces and return them to the soup. Remove the bouquet garni. Adjust the seasoning with salt to taste. Avoid breaking up the prunes.

6. The soup may be served as it is or with the broth thickened with cornstarch. If you opt for the thickening, dilute the cornstarch in the cold water. Stir the mixture gradually into the hot soup until the desired consistency is achieved; bring the soup briefly back to the simmer before serving.

7. Serve, piping hot, garnished with the parsley.

PREPARATION TIME

12 hours or overnight

COOKING TIME

2¼ hours

TEST KITCHEN NOTES

IT IS MY BELIEF THAT THIS TRADITIONAL "COTTAGE" RECIPE WAS INTENDED TO DEAL WITH THE ROOSTER WHEN HE BEGAN TO OVERSLEEP IN THE MORNING. HOW THE PRUNES CAME INTO THE RECIPE IS A MYSTERY, ALTHOUGH THEY ADD A FINE IRONIC NOTE TO THE BIRD'S FATE. IT IS DIFFICULT TO FIND A TOUGH FOWL IN TODAY'S SUPERMARKET, SO THE COOKING TIME HAS BEEN ADJUSTED ACCORDINGLY; THE ROOSTER HIMSELF WOULD HAVE REQUIRED SEVERAL MORE HOURS WHILE THE LADY OF THE COTTAGE WENT ABOUT HER WASH-DAY DUTIES OR OTHER CHORES. THE RECIPE IS SIMPLICITY ITSELF, ONE LONG SIMMER FROM START TO FINISH.

CARBONNADE À LA FLAMANDE

(Flemish Beef Soup)

SERVES 4

INGREDIENTS

2 pounds (1kg) beef chuck

2 tablespoons (30g) butter

1 small onion, sliced thin

Freshly ground black pepper, to taste

2 cups (500ml) premium dark beer

2 cloves garlic, minced

½ teaspoon salt

½ teaspoon sugar

Bouquet garni (2 tablespoons chopped
     celery tops, 2 tablespoons
     chopped parsley, 2 sprigs fresh
     thyme, 1 bay leaf)

1 to 2 cups (250–500ml)
     Chicken Stock II (page 16)

1 tablespoon (15ml) Worcestershire
     sauce, optional

1. Trim the beef of fat and gristle; cut the lean meat into ½-inch (13mm) cubes. Up to half of the meat may be leftovers: steak, trimmings, or beef boiled for pot-au-feu or stock.

2. Melt the butter in a large saucepan over medium-high heat. Add the onion and sauté for 5 minutes. Stir in the meat and brown it over high heat, about 5 minutes.

3. Add a pinch of pepper, the beer, garlic, salt, sugar, and the bouquet garni. Bring the soup to a boil, reduce the heat, and simmer for 1½ hours, or until the meat is very tender and the soup savory. Add chicken stock or more beer as the liquid boils down.

4. Remove the bouquet garni and adjust the seasoning before serving. If you have used a high proportion of leftover meat, you may wish to add depth to the sauce by adding a tablespoon of Worcestershire sauce.

COOKING TIME

1¾ hours

TEST KITCHEN NOTES

BASED ON A FAMILY RECIPE FOR BELGIAN BEEF STEW, THIS IS THE ARCHETYPAL, HEARTY, MAIN-DISH WINTER SOUP. ALTHOUGH LONG IN THE COOKING, IT IS EXTREMELY SIMPLE TO MAKE AND IS AN EXCELLENT VEHICLE FOR LEFTOVERS. TO MAKE IT EVEN MORE SATISFYING, SERVE WITH POTATO GNOCCHI COOKED SEPARATELY, OR WITH POTATOES, ONE PER SERVING, WHICH MAY BE BOILED SEPARATELY AND CUBED, OR CUBED AND COOKED IN THE SOUP FOR THE LAST 20 MINUTES. THIS HELPS THICKEN THE SOUP.

Gulyas (Goulash) Soup

SERVES 6

INGREDIENTS

3 tablespoons (45ml) bacon fat or oil

1¾ pounds (875g) beef chuck

1 large onion, chopped

4 cups (1L) hot Beef Stock (page 18)

1 green pepper, seeded and diced

1½ cups (375g) coarsely chopped
   fresh or crushed, canned tomatoes

1 clove garlic, minced

1 tablespoon (10g) sweet paprika

1 teaspoon bruised caraway seeds

1 teaspoon salt

6 small potatoes, peeled and cubed

¼ medium cabbage, coarsely chopped

2 carrots, peeled and chopped

1 bay leaf

Salt and freshly ground black pepper

Slivered sweet peppers and sour cream,
   for garnish

1. Melt the bacon fat in a large heavy-bottomed saucepan over medium-high heat. Cut the beef into bite-size cubes and sear it in the hot fat, about 5 minutes. When the meat is browned all over, add the onion. Continue to cook until the onion is soft, stirring occasionally, about 10 minutes.

2. When the onions are translucent, have 2 cups (500ml) of heated stock ready. Add it to the meat with the pepper, tomatoes, garlic, paprika, and caraway seeds. Stir it all together, add salt to taste, bring to a boil, cover, and simmer for 1½ hours, stirring occasionally to prevent sticking, until thickened.

3. Heat the remaining 2 cups (500ml) of stock and add to the soup along with the potatoes, cabbage, carrots, and bay leaf. Cook for 20 minutes more, or until the vegetables are done. You may need at this point to add more stock or tomato juice to bring the soup to the desired consistency. It should remain a fairly thick soup, however. Adjust the seasoning with salt and pepper.

4. Gulyas soup may be served as is, or garnished with slivered sweet peppers and a spoonful of sour cream.

COOKING TIME

2¾ hours

TEST KITCHEN NOTES

IF YOU HAPPEN TO HAVE LEFTOVER GOULASH ON HAND, DILUTE IT CUP FOR CUP WITH BEEF OR CHICKEN STOCK, OR TOMATO JUICE, AND PROCEED WITH STEP **3** ABOVE, ADJUSTING THE SEASONING WITH PAPRIKA AND SALT IF NECESSARY.

POT-AU-FEU

SERVES 4 OR 5

INGREDIENTS

1 pound (500g) beef chuck

1 marrow bone

2 pounds (1kg) beef ribs

2½ quarts (2.5L) cold water

1 tablespoon (10g) salt

Bouquet garni (parsley, bay, thyme,
    and sage or oregano or rosemary)

4 carrots, peeled

4 small turnips, peeled

2 stalks celery

1 large onion, stuck with 1 clove

1 pound (500g) white parts of leeks,
    kept whole

¼ small cabbage, roughly chopped

4-5 potatoes

Horseradish, French mustard,
    French bread, for serving

1. Tie the chuck together with string to avoid disintegration. Wrap the marrow bone in cheesecloth and secure it with string or a rubber band. Place these in a large pot with the beef ribs, cold water, and salt. Bring very slowly to a boil.

2. In the interim, prepare a bouquet garni tied up with string. Add it along with 2 carrots, 2 turnips, the celery, onion, leeks, and cabbage to the soup when it reaches a boil. Cover the pot and simmer for 2½ hours.

3. At the end of this time, remove the limpest of the vegetables and discard them. The carrots and turnips can stay. Remove the marrow bone and all of the beef. Add the potatoes and remaining fresh carrots and turnips. Cover the pot and cook for 30 minutes or until the potatoes are fork-tender.

4. Bone the beef ribs; untie the chuck; cut all of the meat into chunks and return it to the pot for another 15 minutes or so.

5. Before serving, discard the bouquet garni. Remove the vegetables and meat to warmed soup plates and ladle the broth over them separately from a tureen. Serve with horseradish, French mustard, and French bread on the side.

COOKING TIME

3¼ hours

TEST KITCHEN NOTES

THIS IS A TRUE PEASANT "SOUPE" IN THE ORIGINAL SENSE OF THE WORD. I USED TO PREPARE IT USING SHIN OF BEEF OR, BETTER YET, VEAL SHIN, ONE CHUNK PER DINER. HOWEVER, THE BUTCHER NOW CONVERTS ALL HIS BEEF SHINS TO HAMBURGER DURING HALF THE YEAR, SO I EXPERIMENTED WITH OTHER CUTS AND FOUND THESE SATISFACTORY. ANY LEFTOVER BROTH MAY BE STRAINED AND FROZEN FOR USE IN FUTURE SOUPS.

Oxtail Soup

INGREDIENTS

2 pounds (1kg) oxtail

1 tablespoon (15ml) corn oil
   or beef drippings

3 tablespoons (45g) tomato paste

4 cups (1L) Beef Stock (page 18)

1 bay leaf

3 or 4 peppercorns

1 teaspoon salt

12 pearl onions

1 stalk celery, diced

1 carrot, diced

Salt and freshly ground black pepper,
   to taste

1. Preheat oven to 300°F (150°C).

2. Trim excess amounts of fat from the sections of oxtail. Heat the oil in a large, oven-proof, heavy-bottomed pot over medium-high heat. Brown the meat on all sides taking care not to char it. This should take about 15 minutes.

3. While the meat is browning, dilute the tomato paste in the beef stock and warm it to the simmering point. Pour 3 cups (750ml) of the hot stock over the browned meat and add the bay leaf and peppercorns. Bring the soup back to a boil, cover the pot tightly, and place it in the oven to simmer for $2\frac{1}{2}$ to 3 hours. While this method provides more even heat and helps prevent scorching, it also promotes greater evaporation of liquids, so you will need to check the pot occasionally and add broth as necessary.

4. When the meat is tender, strain off the broth and degrease it. Add more stock to make at least 3 cups (750ml) of liquid.

5. Return the broth to the pot. Add the pearl onions, celery, and carrots. Simmer until the vegetables are tender, about 20 minutes.

6. While the vegetables are cooking, bone the meat. Return it to the soup and adjust the seasoning with salt and black pepper.

COOKING TIME

$3\frac{1}{2}$ hours

TEST KITCHEN NOTES

THIS IS A HEARTY, COLD-WEATHER SOUP, SIMPLE BUT INCREDIBLY RICH. SERVE PIPING HOT WITH A SIDE DISH OF SMALL PASTA SUCH AS BOW-TIES, SPIRALS, OR SHELLS; OR WITH GNOCCHI, BOILED POTATOES, OR BARLEY, ALL COOKED SEPARATELY. A SALAD OF MIXED GREENS WITH A FAIRLY TART VINAIGRETTE AND CRUSTY BREAD OR ROLLS PERFECTLY BALANCES THE MEAL.

MULLIGATAWNY SOUP

SERVES 6

INGREDIENTS

4 or 5 cups (1–1.25L) lamb broth (use
    the leftover bones and drippings
    from roasted leg of lamb) or Chicken
    or Beef Stock (pages 16 or 18)

¼ cup (63ml) lamb or chicken fat,
    or butter

½ onion, diced

1 carrot, diced

2 stalks celery with leaves, diced

1 green pepper, seeded and diced

1 clove garlic, minced

2 slices fresh ginger root, or
    1 teaspoon ground ginger

8 grains coriander

1 tablespoon (10g) curry powder,
    or more, to taste

¼ cup (35g) flour

1 cup (120g) chopped cooked lamb

1 sprig parsley

1 tart apple, cored, peeled, and diced

1 teaspoon salt, or to taste

Freshly ground black pepper, to taste

Lemon wedges, for garnish

1. To make the lamb broth, cover the disjointed leg with cold water and simmer for about 1 hour, until the meat can be readily pulled from the bones. Set aside the meat and discard the bones.

2. Heat the fat in a large saucepan over medium-high heat. Add the onion, carrot, celery, and green pepper and sauté until the onion is tender but not browned, about 10 minutes.

3. Stir in the garlic, ginger, coriander, and curry powder. Cook and stir for 2 or 3 minutes, then stir in the flour a little at a time, to incorporate. Gradually add the broth, stirring constantly to prevent lumps; add the cooked lamb and the parsley. If you are using leftover roast lamb and have juices or gravy, add them at this time. Simmer for 15 minutes.

4. Add the apple; continue to cook for 15 minutes. Adjust seasoning with salt and pepper.

5. Serve hot, garnished with lemon wedges especially if you have chosen to add extra curry powder for a spicier soup.

COOKING TIME

1¾ hours

TEST KITCHEN NOTES

THIS WAS ORIGINALLY A PAKISTANI DISH, WHICH ACCOUNTS FOR THE EXOTIC SPICES. IT IS PROBABLY MOST OFTEN MADE WITH COOKED CHICKEN AND CHICKEN STOCK, ALTHOUGH I PREFER THE LAMB. IF YOU ARE USING UNCOOKED CHICKEN, CUT IT UP AND ADD IT AT THE SAME TIME AS THE BROTH.

FOR AN EVEN MORE SUBSTANTIAL SOUP, SERVE WITH WHITE RICE ON THE SIDE, TO BE STIRRED INTO THE SOUP.

DUTCH SPLIT PEA SOUP

INGREDIENTS

1 pound (500g) green split peas, picked
    over and rinsed
¼ pound (125g) salt pork, minced
2 medium onions, diced fine
1 carrot, diced fine
2 stalks celery with leaves, diced fine
1 ham bone (or 2 ham hocks
    or a lamb bone)
8 cups (2L) water, or Chicken Stock II
    (page 16) if you have no meaty
    bones to flavor the soup
8 sprigs parsley, minced
2 cloves garlic, minced
2 sprigs thyme, or ¼ teaspoon dried
1 bay leaf
1 whole jalapeño pepper,
    stem removed and seeded
1 pound (500g) cubed ham, optional
Salt and freshly ground black pepper

1. Place the peas in a large bowl, cover with cold water, and soak overnight. Drain and rinse the peas before using. (Or if you are in a rush, put the peas in a saucepan with plenty of water, bring to a boil, and remove from the heat. Let stand for 1 hour, drain, and rinse again.)

2. Toss the salt pork into a large heavy saucepan over medium-high heat and sauté until golden, about 10 minutes. Set aside the pork scraps for use as garnish.

3. Sauté the onions, carrot, and celery in the pork fat over medium heat until tender but not browned, about 10 minutes.

4. If you have a meaty ham or lamb bone, add it to the vegetables with the water. If you are using ham hocks instead, add them and use half water and half chicken or beef stock as the liquid.

5. Add the parsley, garlic, thyme, bay leaf, peas, and the jalapeño to the soup.

6. Bring the soup to a boil, reduce the heat, and simmer for about 1 hour, or until the peas disintegrate. At this time remove the bones from the soup, cool sufficiently to handle, and pick the meat from the bones. Return the meat to the soup to reheat. If you used ham hocks, you may extract what meat you can from them at this time, which will be precious little. Add the optional ham at this time and reheat.

7. Discard the jalapeño and adjust the seasoning with salt and pepper. Serve garnished with the fried salt pork bits.

SOAKING TIME

overnight or at least 1 hour

COOKING TIME

1½ hours

TEST KITCHEN NOTES

THERE ARE MYRIAD VARIATIONS ON THE THEME OF PEA SOUP: YOU CAN EVEN MAKE IT WITH A CHICKEN OR TURKEY CARCASS, THE SMOKED VARIETY BEING PARTICULARLY TASTY. IN ANY CASE, I ALWAYS SERVE IT WITH CORNBREAD, CORNMEAL MUFFINS, OR A SPICY CORNMEAL CASSEROLE. A TOMATO OR GREEK SALAD COMPLETES THE MEAL WONDERFULLY.

PEA SOUP WITH SHRIMP

INGREDIENTS

½ pound (250g) yellow or green
split peas, picked over and rinsed

2 tablespoons (30ml) olive oil

½ carrot, peeled and chopped

1 stalk celery with leaves, chopped

1 medium leek, white part only,
well-rinsed and chopped fine

3 cups (750ml) Chicken Stock II
(page 16)

3 sprigs parsley, chopped fine

1 bay leaf

1 sprig fresh thyme, or ⅛ teaspoon dried

¼ teaspoon curry powder,
or more to taste

½ pound (250g) small fresh shrimp

¼ pound (125g) monkfish

Juice of ½ lemon

1 cup (250ml) dry white wine

Salt and freshly ground black pepper,
to taste

2 cups (250g) Herbed Croutons
(page 11), for garnish

1. Cover the peas with cold water and soak overnight. Drain and rinse the peas before using. (Or if you are in a rush, put the peas in a saucepan with plenty of water, bring to a boil, remove from the heat, and let stand for 1 hour. Drain and rinse the peas before using.)

2. Heat the olive oil in a large saucepan over medium-high heat. Add the carrot, celery, and leek and sauté in the olive oil until tender but not browned, about 10 minutes.

3. Add the chicken stock and the peas. Stir in the parsley, bay leaf, thyme, and curry powder. Bring to a boil, reduce the heat, and simmer for 1 hour or until the peas disintegrate.

4. While the peas are cooking, prepare the seafood: peel and devein the shrimp and cut in half lengthwise. Cut the monkfish into bite-size pieces. Mix the fish and shrimp in a small bowl with the lemon juice. Cover and let stand in the refrigerator for 1 hour.

5. Bring the white wine to a simmer in a small saucepan. Add the marinated seafood, simmer for 2 or 3 minutes, then add both the seafood and the cooking liquid to the pea soup. Adjust seasoning with salt and pepper to taste.

6. Serve piping hot, garnished with croutons.

SOAKING TIME

overnight or at least 1 hour

COOKING TIME

1¼ hours

TEST KITCHEN NOTES

THE COMBINATION OF MONKFISH AND SHRIMP WORKS VERY WELL IN THIS SOMEWHAT REFINED PEA SOUP, BUT BAY SCALLOPS AND CRAB MEAT ARE ALSO SUITABLE. MIX AND MATCH, BUT DON'T USE TOO MANY DIFFERENT VARIETIES AT ONCE.

PEANUT, PORK, AND EGGPLANT SOUP

SERVES 6

INGREDIENTS

¼ cup (30g) flour

4 tablespoons (35g) chopped cilantro
   (reserve 2 tablespoons for garnish)

½ teaspoon salt

Pinch cayenne

1 pound (500g) boneless
   loin of pork, cubed

4 tablespoons (60ml) vegetable oil

4 cups (1L) Chicken Stock I (page 15)

Pinch salt

1 whole jalapeño pepper, stemmed
   and seeded, or freshly ground
   black pepper, to taste

1 large onion, chopped

½ large eggplant, chopped

10 cloves garlic, peeled

1 cup (250g) natural peanut butter
   (no additives)

1 large tomato, coarsely chopped,
   or 1 cup (240g) canned crushed
   tomatoes

½ cup (60g) loosely packed fresh
   sorrel (or cress or spinach), sliced
   into thin strips

2 medium potatoes, peeled and
   boiled, then cubed

Freshly ground black pepper, to taste

1. On a sheet of wax paper, thoroughly combine the flour, salt, 2 tablespoons of the chopped cilantro, and the cayenne.

2. Dredge the pork in the seasoned flour. Heat 2 tablespoons (30ml) of oil in a large saucepan over high heat and quickly brown the meat in it. Add the chicken stock, a little salt, and the jalapeño or black pepper. Bring to a boil, cover, and simmer for 30 minutes.

3. Heat the remaining 2 tablespoons (30ml) of vegetable oil in a medium saucepan over low heat. Add the onion, eggplant, and garlic and cook until tender but not browned, about 15 minutes. Set aside.

4. Stir a little of the hot soup into the peanut butter until a thinner, smooth paste results, then stir the paste into the saucepan. Add the tomato, the reserved vegetables, and the sorrel. Simmer for 15 minutes longer. Add the potatoes and continue to cook for 5 minutes. If the soup seems too thick, dilute with a little of the water the potatoes were cooked in, but keep in mind that it should be a fairly thick and spicy soup. Discard the jalapeño and adjust the seasoning accordingly with salt and pepper.

5. Serve, garnished with the reserved chopped cilantro (you may substitute chopped parsley).

COOKING TIME

55 minutes

TEST KITCHEN NOTES

PEANUT SAUCES AND SOUPS ARE ALWAYS HEARTY, AND IN WEST AFRICA THEY ARE OFTEN DOWNRIGHT FIERY, TOO. THE HEAT OF THE JALAPEÑO DEVELOPS GRADUALLY, SO DON'T OVERDO THE PEPPERING. IT CAN CATCH UP WITH YOU, AND WILL OVERWHELM THE EGGPLANT WHEN IT DOES. A GREEN SALAD MAKES A GOOD ACCOMPANIMENT TO THIS FLAVORFUL SOUP.

Zuppa di Ceci Avantagiatta

(Quick Chick Pea Soup)

INGREDIENTS

½ pound (250g) dried or 1 19-ounce
    (538g) can chick peas
1 ounce (30g) dried porcini mushrooms
3 cups (750ml) lukewarm water
3 tablespoons (45ml) extra-virgin
    olive oil
2 onions, chopped
2½ ounces (75g) pancetta or lean salt
    pork, cut into thin strips
1 carrot, peeled and chopped
1 stalk celery with leaves, chopped
2 teaspoons (10ml) tomato paste
3 cups (750ml) Chicken Stock II
    (page 16)
Salt and freshly ground black pepper,
    to taste
¼ cup (30g) grated Parmesan cheese

1. If you use dried chick peas, rinse them thoroughly in a colander, then cover with 2 inches (5cm) cold water and soak overnight. Transfer the chick peas with their water to a saucepan and boil for 30 minutes or until tender. Drain and rinse before adding to the soup. (Or if you are in a rush, put them in a saucepan with water to cover by 2 inches [5cm]. Bring to a boil, reduce the heat, and simmer about 40 minutes or until tender; drain and rinse.) If you are using canned chick peas, drain and rinse them. Set aside.

2. Rinse the mushrooms then soak in the lukewarm water for at least 30 minutes. Agitate them at the end of soaking to loosen any remaining grit; using a slotted spoon, lift out the mushrooms. Chop and set aside. Strain the soaking liquid through a dampened, wrung-out cheesecloth and reserve.

3. Heat the olive oil in a heavy saucepan over medium heat, then add the onions and pancetta. Cook and stir until the onions are translucent, about 10 minutes, then add the carrot and celery. Continue to cook, stirring occasionally, for about 20 minutes longer or until the vegetables are tender and lightly browned.

4. Dissolve the tomato paste in the mushroom water; add this mixture to the vegetables and continue cooking until all the liquid has boiled away, about 15 minutes.

5. Add the chick peas and stock to the vegetables. Simmer for 10 minutes, then adjust the seasoning with salt and pepper.

6. Serve with toasted slices of crusty bread, with Parmesan cheese handed around separately.

SOAKING TIME

overnight or at least 1 hour

COOKING TIME

1½ hours

TEST KITCHEN NOTES

THIS SOUP IS ONLY QUICK IF YOU USE CANNED CHICK PEAS. IF, LIKE ME, YOU PREFER TO STOCK THE DRIED VARIETY, IT IS IMPORTANT TO PLAN AHEAD.

FOR THE AMOUNT OF TIME REQUIRED TO ACTUALLY COOK IT, THIS SOUP HAS AN ASTOUNDINGLY RICH FLAVOR, DUE TO THE USE OF THE REDUCED MUSHROOM WATER. ALTHOUGH HEARTY AND SATISFYING AS IT IS, YOU MAY ADD A LITTLE COOKED CUBED HAM BEFORE SERVING IF YOU PREFER A MEATIER MAIN DISH. BE CAREFUL OF THE SALT CONTENT OF THE HAM IF YOU DO.

TURKEY SOUP WITH DUMPLINGS

SERVES 6

INGREDIENTS

Turkey carcass, including neck
    and giblets
6 cups (1.5L) cold water or Vegetable
    Broth (page 20)
2 medium onions, quartered
2½ stalks celery with leaves
6 peppercorns
Bouquet garni (bay leaf, thyme,
    rosemary, oregano)
2 carrots, peeled and sliced
1 pound (500g) leftover turkey meat,
    optional
Salt and freshly ground black pepper,
    to taste
½ cup (90g) green peas
Dumpling batter (page 13)

1. If the neck and giblets are not yet cooked, put them in a small saucepan, barely cover with cold water, and bring to a boil and simmer for 45 minutes.

2. Break down the turkey carcass in small components. While you are doing this, pull off any large pieces of meat and set aside. If your bird was smoked, remove and discard the skin to avoid overwhelming the turkey flavor. (There will inevitably be some smoky flavor to your broth, but removing the skin helps keep the smokiness to an acceptable level.)

3. Place the turkey in a stock pot with the partially cooked giblets and their water, the cold water, onions, celery, and peppercorns. Add the bouquet garni, keeping in mind that the stock will also be flavored by the herbs used in cooking the turkey and the stuffing. Bring slowly to a boil, reduce the heat, cover, and simmer until the meat falls from the bones, about 45 minutes. After the first 30 minutes, add the carrots.

4. After 45 minutes, strain off the stock into a large pot with a tight-fitting lid. Add to it the cooked carrots, any good pieces of meat left among the bones, and the giblets, cubed. Discard the onions, celery, bouquet garni, and bones. If the meat is skimpy, cube and add any leftover turkey that was not included in the stock. Taste and correct the seasoning with salt and pepper (you will not be able to do this once you put in the dumplings).

5. Add the peas and bring the soup to a simmer. Drop in the dumpling batter by tablespoonfuls so that the dumplings do not touch. Cover and let simmer gently for 10 minutes. If you can't stand the suspense, you may use a slotted spoon to flip over the dumplings after 5 minutes, then cook 5 minutes longer. Test the dumplings for doneness with a wooden toothpick: if it comes out clean, they're done. Serve at once; dumplings are not very resilient.

COOKING TIME

1¾ hours, including precooking
    the giblets

TEST KITCHEN NOTES

TURKEY SOUP IS A MOST INDIVIDUAL MATTER, SO FEEL FREE TO MAKE THIS RECIPE YOUR OWN BY CHOOSING THE HERBS, VEGETABLES, AND ACCOMPANIMENTS YOU FANCY. IF DUMPLINGS ARE NOT FOR YOU, USE POTATOES, PASTA, OR RICE, REMEMBERING TO PRECOOK THE LATTER TWO BEFORE ADDING. YOUR SOUP OF LEFTOVERS WILL BECOME AN EAGERLY AWAITED TRADITION IN ITS OWN RIGHT.

BRUNSWICK STEW

INGREDIENTS

1 3-pound (1.5kg) chicken

2 tablespoons (30ml) butter or corn oil

1 pound (500g) lean pork, cubed

2 medium onions, chopped

2 pounds (1kg) chopped fresh or canned
    crushed tomatoes

4 medium potatoes, peeled and cubed

2 cups (360g) lima beans,
    frozen or canned

2 cups (360g) corn, frozen or canned

4 teaspoons (20ml) Worcestershire sauce

Salt and freshly ground black pepper,
    to taste

1. Cut up the chicken and put it in a saucepan with enough cold water to cover. Bring very slowly to a boil, cover the pot, and simmer until the meat falls from the bones, 45 minutes to 1 hour. When the chicken is tender, strain off and reserve the broth. Skin, bone, and cube the meat and set aside.

2. While the chicken is cooking, heat the butter or oil in a heavy saucepan over medium-high heat. Sauté the pork and onions until browned, about 15 minutes. Add the tomatoes and potatoes and simmer until the potatoes are tender, about 15 minutes, taking care not to scorch either vegetable.

3. Add the lima beans, corn, and reserved chicken stock and cook until the beans and pork are fork-tender, about 15 minutes. At this point, add the reserved chicken meat. Stir in the Worcestershire sauce. Adjust the seasoning with salt and pepper. Cook until the chicken is heated through.

COOKING TIME

1½ hours

TEST KITCHEN NOTES

IN SPITE OF ITS NAME THIS IS TRULY A SOUP, ALBEIT A THICK ONE. SOME RECIPES DO INDEED REQUIRE "SEVERAL HOURS," OR "FOUR TO FIVE HOURS," OF COOKING UNTIL IT IS POSSIBLE TO EAT THE DISH WITH A FORK, AND IF YOU USE A STEWING HEN (AND/OR THE RABBIT OR SQUIRREL RECOMMENDED IN OLD COOKBOOKS), THE COOKING WILL NECESSARILY BE LONG. BUT WE HAVE CHOSEN A MODERN VERSION OF THIS CLASSIC SOUTHERN DISH INVOLVING NOTHING MORE EXOTIC THAN THE EVERYDAY FRYER AND LEAN PORK. THE USE OF FROZEN AND CANNED VEGETABLES ALSO SPEEDS THE COOKING PROCESS, PUTTING THIS PLAIN, DOWN-HOME DISH ON YOUR TABLE IN RECORD TIME. HOT CORNBREAD MAKES AN EXCELLENT ACCOMPANIMENT TO THIS HEARTY SOUP.

ARAN SCALLOP SOUP

INGREDIENTS

1 leek

2 small onions, chopped

1 stalk celery, diced

½ pound (250g) mushrooms

1½ pounds (750g) tomatoes

6 ounces (175g) lean bacon or
    salt pork, diced

6 tablespoons (90g) butter

4 cups (1L) bottled clam juice

3 cups (750ml) water

Freshly ground black pepper, to taste

Bouquet garni (3 sprigs each of parsley
    and fresh thyme)

2 pounds (1kg) potatoes,
    peeled and diced

2 pounds (1kg) sea scallops, drained
    and cut in quarters, or bay scallops,
    left whole

1 to 1½ cups (250–375ml) heavy cream

Salt, to taste

Pinch cayenne

Beurre manié, optional (page 124)

1. Remove the green portion of the leek, cut the white part in half lengthwise, separate the layers and rinse carefully to remove any grit, and pat dry and slice thin. Put the onions and celery in a bowl with the leeks. Clean the mushrooms with as little exposure to water as possible (pat clean with a damp paper towel) and slice thinly, then set aside with the other vegetables. Bring a small saucepan of water to a boil and place the tomatoes in it for a few minutes, until the skins split. Quickly run each tomato under cold water for ease in handling, then slip off the skins. Remove the stem ends, chop the flesh, and add the tomatoes to the vegetable bowl.

2. Lightly brown the bacon or salt pork in a heavy-bottomed saucepan over medium heat, about 10 minutes. Pour off the excess fat and add the butter and the reserved vegetables. Cook and stir over low heat for 5 minutes, then add the clam juice, water, pepper, and the bouquet garni. Bring the soup to a boil, then simmer over low heat for about 30 minutes, stirring occasionally.

3. Add the potatoes and cook for 20 minutes more.

4. If you are ready to sit down and eat, add the scallops and cook for 10 minutes at this point. It is important not to overcook these luscious little morsels, so take a break in the cooking process until you are almost ready to serve. In either case, when the scallops are just barely opaque, discard the bouquet garni and add the cream. Adjust the seasoning, adding salt and a tiny pinch of cayenne. Bring the soup to serving temperature. If you wish to have a slightly thicker consistency, have a small amount of beurre manié ready and add it carefully at this time.

COOKING TIME

1 hour

TEST KITCHEN NOTES

HAD IT ORIGINATED IN THE UNITED STATES, THIS SOUP WOULD SURELY HAVE BEEN CALLED A CHOWDER. ALTHOUGH I WAS AT FIRST LOATH TO PUT "REAL" SCALLOPS INTO A SOUP, IT WAS WORTH IT: THIS IS ONE OF THE GREAT SOUPS, BOTH ELEGANT AND SATISFYING. IF YOU CANNOT FIND CLAM JUICE, YOU MAY SUBSTITUTE FUMET (PAGE 21).

BEURRE MANIÉ IS GOOD TO HAVE ON HAND, AND MAKING IT IS SIMPLE. USE SPARINGLY, A SMALL BIT AT A TIME, TO THICKEN SOUPS; YOU'LL BE AMAZED AT HOW EFFECTIVE IT IS.

MANHATTAN CLAM CHOWDER

INGREDIENTS

¼ pound (125g) salt pork, minced

1 medium onion, diced

1 stalk celery, diced

1 pound (500g) clams, shucked and
    minced fine

½ green pepper, stemmed, seeded,
    and diced

2 medium potatoes, peeled and cubed

2 cups (480g) chopped fresh
    or canned crushed tomatoes

1 bay leaf

2 cups (500ml) water

2 tablespoons (30g) tomato paste

Salt and freshly ground black pepper,
    to taste

½ teaspoon (2.25ml) Worcestershire
    sauce, optional

Oyster crackers or Croutons (page 11),
    for garnish

1. Sauté the salt pork in a large saucepan over medium heat until golden and all the fat is rendered out, about 10 minutes. Remove the bits and reserve in a safe place.

2. Gently cook the onion and celery in the pork fat until translucent, about 10 minutes.

3. Add the clams to the vegetables and cook, stirring, for about 5 minutes.

4. Add the green pepper and potato to the clam mixture. Add the tomatoes, bay leaf, and the water and bring soup to a boil. Immediately reduce the heat and simmer until the potatoes are cooked but still firm, about 10 to 15 minutes.

5. Add the tomato paste. Adjust the seasoning with salt and pepper. Add the Worcestershire sauce if desired. Bring just to a simmer, remove from the heat, and refrigerate several hours or overnight for the flavors to develop.

6. Remove the bay leaf and heat to serving temperature. Garnish with the reserved salt pork bits and oyster crackers or croutons.

COOKING TIME

40 minutes

STANDING TIME

3–4 hours or overnight

TEST KITCHEN NOTES

THIS IS THE "OTHER" CHOWDER, AND I AM WILLING TO GRANT THAT IT IS A MORE ROBUST ONE, PRACTICALLY A STEW. AS WITH THE NEW ENGLAND CLAM CHOWDER (PAGE 63), THE FLAVOR-DEVELOPMENT PERIOD IS ESSENTIAL: PREPARE IT THE NIGHT BEFORE OR IN THE MORNING FOR THAT DAY'S DINNER, REFRIGERATING THE STANDING CHOWDER.

CAJUN OYSTER CHOWDER

SERVES 8

INGREDIENTS

½ pound (250g) salt pork, diced small

2 stalks celery, diced

2 medium onions, chopped

2 or 3 medium potatoes, peeled
    and cubed

1 large green pepper, stemmed,
    seeded, and diced

1 bay leaf

¼ teaspoon dried sage or rosemary

¼ teaspoon dried thyme

3 cloves garlic, minced

⅛ teaspoon cayenne, or to taste

2⅓ cups (583ml) water

¼ cup (35g) flour

3 cups (750ml) whole milk

1 pound (500g) fresh oysters, shucked,
    their liquor reserved

Croutons toasted with olive oil (page 11)
    and chopped scallion greens and
    parsley, for garnish

1. Sauté the diced salt pork in a large saucepan over medium heat until lightly browned, about 10 minutes. Remove the pork bits and set aside.

2. Add the celery and onions to the pork fat and cook over medium-high heat until lightly browned, about 10 minutes.

3. Stir the potatoes and green peppers into the vegetables, then add the bay leaf, sage, thyme, garlic, cayenne, and water. Bring to a boil; immediately reduce the heat and simmer until the potatoes are tender, about 10 to 15 minutes.

4. Put the flour in a small bowl, then gradually stir in ½ cup (125ml) milk to make a smooth paste. Blend this mixture into the chowder, then add the rest of the milk and return to a boil, stirring constantly. Simmer for 5 minutes, then add the oysters and their liquor; bring just to a boil and then remove from the heat.

5. Although you may serve this spicy chowder straight away, it is better if it stands, covered and refrigerated, for 3 or 4 hours or even overnight to allow the flavors to blend. Just before serving, remove the bay leaf, bring the chowder back to a simmer, and add the fried pork bits.

6. Garnish with croutons and a sprinkling of chopped scallion greens and parsley.

COOKING TIME

40 minutes

STANDING TIME

3–4 hours or overnight

TEST KITCHEN NOTES

THIS IS A GUTSY CHOWDER. IF YOU LET IT STAND, USE THE CAYENNE WITH CAUTION AS ITS FLAVOR DEEPENS SIGNIFICANTLY.

ON THE SUBJECT OF SALT PORK, THERE ARE TWO WAYS TO TREAT IT: AFTER BROWNING, LEAVE IT IN THE SOUP FOR THE FULL COOKING TIME, WHICH SOFTENS THE PORK AND MAKES IT LOSE ITS CHARACTER; OR REMOVE IT, LEAVING IT VULNERABLE TO KITCHEN PREDATORS (AMONG THEM THE COOK). IN THE LATTER CASE, COVER AND PROTECT THOSE BITS, BUT DON'T FORGET TO RETURN THEM TO THE SOUP JUST BEFORE SERVING; YOU MAY ALSO HAND THEM AROUND SEPARATELY AS AN ADDITIONAL GARNISH.

CHICKEN GUMBO

INGREDIENTS

1 3- to 4-pound (1.5–2kg) chicken
3 to 4 tablespoons (30–40g) Creole
    seasoning
2 tablespoons (30ml) bacon fat
1 ham hock, or 1 pound (500g) smoked
    or andouille sausage
2 cups (500ml) boiling water
1 green pepper, seeded and diced
2 stalks celery with leaves, chopped
5 cloves garlic, crushed
2 tomatoes, chopped
1 small onion, diced
1 cup (180g) sliced okra (about 6),
    cut into ¼-inch (7mm) slices
4 cups (1L) cold water
1 cup (180g) fresh corn kernels, optional
2 tablespoons chopped parsley
2 teaspoons (10ml) Worcestershire sauce
½ teaspoon filé powder
3 cups (450g) cooked white rice
Chopped scallions, for garnish

1. Cut up the chicken and sprinkle the pieces with Creole seasoning. In a large saucepan over medium heat, brown the chicken quickly in the bacon fat. Once browned, add the ham hock and boiling water, then cover and simmer until the chicken falls from the bone, about 1 hour.

2. While the chicken is cooking, clean and prepare the vegetables. Place the green pepper, celery, garlic, tomatoes, onions, and okra in a pot with the cold water, bring to a boil, and simmer until tender, about 30 minutes.

3. When the chicken is done, remove the meat from the stock. Discard the skin and bones and chop the meat. Return the chicken to the stock, add the vegetables with their stock and the corn, if you are using it. Bring to a boil, then remove from the heat and stir in the parsley and Worcestershire sauce. Let the gumbo stand, covered, for at least 1 hour.

4. When ready to serve, bring the gumbo back to a boil. Remove from the heat and stir in the filé powder. Serve it in a soup plate over ½ cup (75g) white rice. Garnish with scallions.

COOKING TIME

1¼ hours

STANDING TIME

1 hour

TEST KITCHEN NOTES

CLASSIC GUMBOS CAN BE VERY SPICY, ALMOST ALWAYS INCLUDE OKRA (WHICH ARE SOMETIMES ACTUALLY CALLED "GUMBOS" IN SOME LANGUAGES), AND ARE FINISHED OFF WITH FILÉ POWDER. UNLIKE SOME GUMBO RECIPES, THIS ONE DOES NOT INCLUDE A ROUX.

FILÉ IS MADE FROM THE LEAVES OF THE SASSAFRAS TREE, SUPPOSEDLY HARVESTED DURING THE AUGUST FULL MOON, THEN DRIED AND GROUND TO A POWDER. WHEN USED IN THE COOKING PROCESS, IT ACTS AS A THICKENER FOR THE SOUP AS WELL AS A FLAVORING. BE SURE TO ADD IT AT THE VERY END OF COOKING, SINCE IT CAN BECOME STRINGY AND TOUGH WHEN EXPOSED TO HEAT.

DOMINO SOUP

SERVES 8

INGREDIENTS

1 pound (500g) dried black beans

1 pound (500g) squid, diced into ¼-inch
   (7mm) pieces

½ cup (125ml) freshly squeezed
   lemon juice

1 large onion, chopped

2 cloves garlic, minced

2 carrots, peeled and diced

2 stalks celery, diced

1 green pepper, stemmed, seeded,
   and diced

1 or 2 smoked ham hocks

1 sprig thyme, or ½ teaspoon dried

1 bay leaf

½ teaspoon mace

4 cups (1L) Chicken Stock II (page 16)

4 cups (1L) water

Salt and freshly ground black pepper,
   to taste

½ teaspoon sugar

Pinch cayenne

½ cup (125ml) dry sherry

1. Pick over the beans, removing any foreign matter. Soak overnight; or if you're in a rush, place in a large saucepan covered with at least 2 inches (5cm) of water, bring to a boil, and cook for 2 minutes. Remove from the heat, cover, and soak for 1 hour. Whichever method you use, drain the beans and rinse with cold water before proceeding.

2. Place the squid in a bowl with lemon juice to marinate. Stir occasionally while the rest of the soup is cooking.

3. Place the onion, garlic, carrots, celery, and pepper in a large pot with the beans, ham hock(s), thyme, bay leaf, mace, chicken stock, and water. Bring to a boil, reduce the heat, and simmer for 1½ hours, or until the beans are quite tender.

4. Remove the ham hock(s) and bay leaf; pick off any meat, then chop it and set aside.

5. Set aside a cup (180g) or so of the beans to provide texture to the soup, then purée the contents of the pot in a blender or food processor, or put through a food mill. Return the puréed soup to the pot, adding the reserved beans and the ham. Season to taste with salt and pepper. Add the sugar and cayenne.

6. When ready to serve, bring the soup back to a boil, stir in the marinated squid with its lemon juice, and the sherry; heat until piping hot and serve immediately.

SOAKING TIME

overnight or at least 1 hour

COOKING TIME

about 2 hours

TEST KITCHEN NOTES

IF SQUID IS NOT TO YOUR TASTE, THE "DOMINO" SPOTS IN THIS RICH, HEARTY SOUP MAY BE PROVIDED BY SMALL CUBES OF MONKFISH, SHRIMP, OR EVEN LOBSTER. MARINATE THE SEAFOOD IN THE LEMON JUICE FOLLOWING THE INSTRUCTIONS FOR THE SQUID. TO ROUND OUT THIS DISH, SERVE WITH BRUSCHETTAS AND A SALAD.

Russian Shchi
(Cabbage Soup)

INGREDIENTS

FOR THE MUSHROOM STOCK

1 ounce (30g) dried wild mushrooms, rinsed
½ medium onion, peeled
4 cups (1L) water

FOR THE BEEF STOCK

1½ pounds (750g) beef chuck
1 marrow bone
8 cups (2L) cold water
1 small carrot, peeled
½ small turnip, peeled
½ parsnip, peeled
1 stalk celery with leaves
2 parsley sprigs
1 leek, white part only, carefully cleaned,
     halved lengthwise and diced
1 sprig of dill
½ teaspoon salt

FOR THE SHCHI

1 pound (500g) sauerkraut
3 tablespoons (45g) butter
1 onion, minced
4 teaspoons flour
5 small potatoes, peeled
1 bay leaf
8 peppercorns
Salt, to taste
1 cup (250ml) sour cream, for garnish

1. Make the mushroom stock: Place the mushrooms, onion, and water in a saucepan. Cover and simmer 2 hours, then drain, reserving the liquid and the mushrooms separately.

2. While the mushroom stock is simmering, make the beef stock: Place the chuck and marrow bone in a stock pot with the cold water and bring to a boil; turn down the heat so you can skim the surface, then add an ice cube, and return to a boil. Repeat the process, add the remaining stock ingredients, and return to a boil. Simmer for 2 hours, partly covered. Strain and reserve the stock and meat separately. Degrease the stock. You should have about 4 cups (1L).

3. Make the shchi: Drain the sauerkraut thoroughly, reserving the liquid to adjust the acidity of the finished soup as necessary.

4. Melt 1 tablespoon (15ml) butter in a large saucepan over medium heat. Sauté the onion gently in the butter until translucent but not browned, about 10 minutes. Add the sauerkraut; heat, stirring constantly.

5. In a separate saucepan over medium heat, melt the remaining 2 tablespoons (30ml) of butter and add the flour, stirring constantly. Gradually add 1½ cups (375ml) of mushroom stock.

6. Stir the flour mixture into the sauerkraut. Add 4 cups (1L) of the beef stock, the potatoes, bay leaf, peppercorns, and salt to taste. Simmer about 45 minutes.

7. While the shchi is simmering, cube the meat reserved from the stock-making. If desired, you may cut up a few of the mushrooms from the mushroom stock and add them to the soup with the cubed meat. Add these ingredients and adjust the seasoning. Remove the bay leaf. If the shchi does not seem tart enough, add some of the reserved sauerkraut juices, to taste.

8. Serve the shchi piping hot, garnished with sour cream, making sure to place one potato in each bowl.

COOKING TIME

About 3 hours

TEST KITCHEN NOTES

YOU MAY SUBSTITUTE A COMMERCIAL BROTH IN THE INTERESTS OF SAVING TIME. YOU WILL THEN HAVE TO SAUTÉ 1 POUND (500G) OR SO OF TENDER CUBED BEEF TO REPLACE THE BOILED BEEF. CHUNKS OF CABBAGE CAN BE SUBSTITUTED FOR THE SAUERKRAUT IF YOU ADD 2 OR 3 SLICED TOMATOES (FOR ACIDITY) IN THE LAST 10 TO 15 MINUTES OF COOKING.

BOUILLABAISSE

SERVES 8 TO 10

FOR THE AIOLI

1 or 2 slices white bread, crusts removed

1 cup (250ml) milk

6 cloves garlic, peeled

2 egg yolks

½ teaspoon salt

1¼ cups (313ml) olive oil

Lemon juice, to taste

FOR THE BOUILLABAISSE

2 leeks, white part only,
    thoroughly cleaned and diced

2 large onions, diced

2 medium tomatoes, cored and diced

2 cloves garlic (or more, to taste), minced

1¼ cups (313ml) olive oil

6 to 8 kinds of fish—4 to 5 pounds
    (2–2.5 kg)—to your taste: for
    shellfish, try langoustine or lobster
    tail, shrimp, mussels, or clams;
    as for for finned fish, try monkfish,
    snapper, croaker, flounder, rockfish,
    whiting, or sea bass

Salt and freshly ground black pepper,
    to taste

Pinch saffron

Croutons (page 11), for garnish

1. Make the aioli: Soak the bread in the milk; after a few minutes, squeeze out all excess moisture from the bread. You should have an egg-sized lump. Place the bread in a mortar with the garlic and pound to a paste.

2. Transfer to a food processor, add the egg yolks, one at a time, then the salt, processing for 30 seconds or so.

3. Drizzle ¼ cup (63ml) of the olive oil very slowly into the egg mixture, processing constantly, over a period of 2 minutes. Add the remaining cup of oil by the same method, over a period of an additional 2 minutes.

4. When you achieve a mayonnaise consistency, taste and adjust the seasoning, processing with a squirt or two of lemon juice, to taste. Set aside.

5. Make the bouillabaisse: Put the leeks, onions, tomatoes, and garlic in a large soup pot with ¼ cup (63ml) of the olive oil and cook slowly, without browning, until the tomatoes disintegrate, about 10 or 15 minutes.

6. When preparing the fish, you may wish to cut the bodies into 3-inch (7.5cm) chunks, but I prefer to leave them whole to prevent disintegration. Cut lobster tails in serving-size chunks; scrub shellfish thoroughly.

7. When the vegetables are done, lay the fish requiring the longest cooking time (such as the monkfish or sea bass) on top, cover with cold water, add salt and pepper and a good pinch of saffron, plus the remaining 1 cup (250ml) of olive oil. Cover the pot, bring to a boil, then simmer for 10 minutes. Add the more fragile fish (such as flounder or whiting) with the clams or mussels; cover and cook just until the shells open.

8. Transfer the fish carefully to a platter. Strain the broth and set it out separately in a tureen. Serve the fish from the platter to soup plates, ladling the broth over all.

9. On the side, or floating in the broth, serve croutons topped with aioli.

COOKING TIME

About 30 minutes

TEST KITCHEN NOTES

THE FISH NECESSARY FOR AUTHENTIC MEDITERRANEAN BOUILLABAISSE DO NOT TRAVEL WELL AND ARE NOT AVAILABLE ELSEWHERE. HOWEVER, YOUR SOUP WILL BE DELICIOUS IF YOU INSIST ON FRESH OCEAN FISH.

AIOLI IS TRADITIONALLY MADE IN A MORTAR, WHICH CAN BE TEDIOUS AND DOESN'T ALWAYS "TAKE." THE FOOD PROCESSOR GUARANTEES SUCCESS AND IS MUCH LESS TIRING.

UKRAINIAN BORSCH

INGREDIENTS

FOR THE KVAS

3 medium beets, peeled and sliced
    very thin
½ pound (250g) very dark rye bread
    (pumpernickel), sliced
2 quarts (2L) water

FOR THE SOUP

1 medium beet, peeled and grated
4 cups (1L) kvas (see Test Kitchen Notes)
2 tablespoons (30g) butter
½ carrot, peeled and grated
½ parsnip, peeled and grated
1 stalk celery, grated
1 medium onion, grated
1 tablespoon (10g) flour
2 medium potatoes, peeled and cubed
½ pound (250g) cabbage, roughly
    shredded
1 bay leaf
Salt and freshly ground black pepper,
    to taste
2 tablespoons (30ml) bacon fat
1 clove garlic, minced
2 plum tomatoes, cut into eighths
Chopped parsley and sour cream,
    for garnish

1. Make the kvas: Layer the beets and bread in a large bowl. Bring the water to a boil and let cool to a lukewarm temperature. Pour over the bread and beets and let stand loosely covered for 3 or 4 days. When it has fermented, you should have a pleasantly acidic liquid for your soup base. Strain through a muslin-lined colander before using. You should have about 5 cups (1.25L) kvas.

2. Make the soup: Place the grated beet in a saucepan with 3 cups (750ml) of kvas (diluted, if you think that the flavor is too strong); bring to a simmer and cook for 30 minutes.

3. Melt the butter in a large saucepan over medium-high heat. Sauté the carrot, parsnip, celery, and onion about 5 minutes. Stir in the flour. Stir in another 1 cup (250ml) of kvas and simmer for 15 minutes.

4. Add the potatoes, cabbage, and beet-kvas mixture to the vegetable-kvas mixture in the large saucepan. Add the bay leaf, salt, and pepper. Simmer 10 to 15 minutes.

5. In a separate saucepan, heat the bacon fat over high heat. Sauté the garlic for 1 or 2 minutes, then add the plum tomatoes and sauté for an additional minute. Add this to the borsch, return to a simmer, and cook gently 15 minutes longer.

6. Serve, topped with a sprinkling of parsley and a dollop of sour cream.

PREPARATION TIME

3 or 4 days

COOKING TIME

1½ hours

TEST KITCHEN NOTES

BORSCH IS ANOTHER OF THOSE "NATIONAL" SOUPS THAT VARY FROM COOK TO COOK AND REGION TO REGION. THIS UKRAINIAN VERSION IS ALMOST WHOLLY VEGETARIAN; RUSSIAN BORSCH CAN BE MADE WITH FRANKFURTERS AND A CHUNK OF HAM. THE LITHUANIAN VERSION IS MADE WITH A LIGHT BEEF STOCK AND BACON, AND THE POLISH, MOST GRANDLY OF ALL, WITH BREAST OF DUCK.

WE ARE TOLD THAT THE "CLASSIC" UKRAINIAN BORSCH CANNOT BE MADE WITHOUT KVAS (AN EASTERN EUROPEAN FERMENTED BEVERAGE), BUT YOU CAN CHEAT A LITTLE. OMIT THE KVAS INGREDIENTS. IN STEP 2, SIMMER THE BEET IN 4 CUPS (1L) OF VEGETABLE STOCK, 2 TABLESPOONS (30G) OF TOMATO PASTE, AND 3 TABLESPOONS (45ML) OF VINEGAR FOR 30 MINUTES OR SO TO APPROXIMATE THE KVAS. IF YOU DO DECIDE TO MAKE AUTHENTIC KVAS, DON'T FORGET TO START DAYS IN ADVANCE.

CREAM CHEESE TARTLETS (PAGE 13) MAKE AN EXCELLENT ACCOMPANIMENT.

CURAÇAO COCONUT SOUP

INGREDIENTS

2 cups (165g) shredded
    unsweetened coconut

2 cups (500ml) milk

6 ounces (175g) chipped beef

4 cups (1L) water

1 onion, chopped fine

2 whole jalapeños (or other small hot
    peppers), stemmed and seeded

1 pound (500g) fish fillet (red snapper,
    mahi mahi, monkfish, etc.)

2 tablespoons (20g) flour

¼ cup (63ml) heavy cream

Juice of ½ lemon

Salt, to taste

1. Stir the coconut and milk together in a saucepan and bring just to a boil over moderate heat. Remove from the heat at once and let stand 30 minutes. Process in a blender to extract the maximum flavor, then press through a strainer. Discard the coconut pulp and set the coconut milk aside.

2. While the coconut is steeping, place the chipped beef, water, onion, and jalapeños in a saucepan, bring to a boil and simmer for 30 minutes.

3. Add the fish and simmer for 20 minutes longer. Remove the skin from the fish, cut the flesh into bite-sized pieces, and set it aside.

4. Stir the flour and heavy cream together in a small bowl.

5. Stir the coconut milk into the soup, then stir in the flour-and-cream mixture. Stirring constantly, bring to a boil, then add the fish again. Cook gently for 5 minutes. Remove the jalapeños and adjust the seasoning with lemon juice and salt. Serve immediately.

STANDING TIME

30 minutes

COOKING TIME

1¼ hours

TEST KITCHEN NOTES

IF CHIPPED BEEF, ONCE SO COMMON, IS NOT AVAILABLE, SUBSTITUTE DICED HAM. DEPENDING ON THE FISH YOU USE, YOU MAY WISH TO INTENSIFY THE FLAVOR BY ADDING A DASH OF WORCESTERSHIRE SAUCE OR AN ORIENTAL FISH SAUCE.

THAI CHICKEN SOUP

INGREDIENTS

3 cups (750ml) Chicken Stock I (page 15)

6 slices peeled fresh ginger or Thai
galangal (see Test Kitchen Notes)

1 stalk lemongrass, bruised and
cut in 2-inch (5cm) pieces

Zest of 1 lime, cut in thin strips
(or 6 to 8 Kaffir lime leaves, bruised)

2 cans Thai coconut milk, about
28 ounces (60ml) total

1 pound (500g) boneless, skinless chicken
breast, diced

½ teaspoon (2g) tamarind paste,
optional

¼ cup (63ml) lime juice

2 tablespoons (20g) light brown sugar

2 tablespoons (30ml) Thai fish sauce
or soy sauce

½ pound (250g) button or enoki
mushrooms

Salt, to taste

Hot red pepper sauce or cayenne,
to taste

1 small fresh hot red pepper or jalapeño,
stemmed, seeded, and sliced thin

1. Place the chicken stock, ginger, lemongrass, and lime zest in a saucepan. Bring to a boil and reduce to 2 cups (500ml).

2. Add the coconut milk, bring to a boil, and let cook 1 minute.

3. Add the chicken, bring to a boil, and cook 2 minutes.

4. Add the tamarind paste, if using, the lime juice, brown sugar, and fish sauce. Stir until well blended.

5. Add the mushrooms: if you are using button mushrooms, slice them thin; if you are able to find enokis, cut off the bottoms of the clusters, then separate the mushrooms by simply pulling them apart. Bring the soup back to a boil and simmer until the mushrooms are tender, about 2 to 3 minutes.

6. Adjust the seasoning: salt to taste (you will find that the Thai fish sauce is very salty), and hot sauce or cayenne for heat. You may wish to remove the ginger slices, lemongrass, and lime peel or leaves before serving.

7. Serve with thin slices of hot red pepper floating on top.

COOKING TIME

45 minutes

TEST KITCHEN NOTES

IF YOU LIVE IN A CITY WITH A SIGNIFICANT ASIAN POPULATION, YOU WILL PROBABLY FIND GALANGAL, FISH SAUCE, KAFFIR LIMES AND THEIR LEAVES, TAMARIND PASTE, AND LEMONGRASS YEAR-ROUND WITHOUT TOO MUCH TROUBLE. FOR THE REST OF US, THIS RECIPE WORKS JUST AS WELL WITH MORE COMMON ALTERNATIVES. IT IS BEAUTIFUL TO LOOK AT AND HEARTY ENOUGH TO SERVE AS A MAIN DISH, PERHAPS WITH A SIDE DISH OF FRIED RICE OR STEAMED STICKY RICE (ANOTHER THAI SPECIALTY) AND A SALAD.

FIRST COURSE SOUPS

Vichyssoise • Carrot Vichyssoise • Jerusalem Artichoke Vichyssoise
Broccoli-Cauliflower Soup • Gazpacho • Chinese Asparagus Soup I
Chinese Asparagus Soup II • Bongo-Bongo Soup • Cream of Tomato Soup
Potage Germiny (Cream of Sorrel Soup) • Cream of Fennel Soup
Cream of Mushroom Soup • Cream of Asparagus Soup • Italian Tomato Soup
Lobster Bisque • Shrimp Bisque • Cauliflower-Caraway Soup • Cucumber Soup
Cold Cantaloupe Soup • Yin and Yang Soup • Avocado Soup
Samoan Coconut Soup

CLEAR GARNISHED SOUPS

Consommé Bellevue • Wonton Soup • Dorothy's Holiday Consommé
Consommé with Diablotins • Consommé Brunoise • Consommé Colbert
Consommé Aurora • Florentine Consommé • Armenian Monti in Broth
Siberian Pel'meni Soup

DESSERT SOUPS

Apricot Soup • Raspberry-Wine Soup • Russian Strawberry Soup
Strawberry Cream Soup • Pumpkin Soup • Honeydew-Citrus Soup
Chilled Port-Plum Soup • Apple-Cranberry Soup
Floating Island • Mixed Fruit Soup

PART THREE

LIGHTER FARE

FIRST COURSE SOUPS

Although this is a book of main course soups, it seems like an oversight not to mention some of the wonderful soups that tend to stand in at the beginning of a meal. Certainly, many of the soups that follow can be turned into main dishes by serving a larger portion. Others are meant to lay the groundwork for the meal ahead, or to whet the palate. Some of the soups are so rich or intense that they cannot be served in large quantities—unless, of course, you are very sure of the appetites of your dining companions.

VICHYSSOISE

SERVES 6

INGREDIENTS

2 leeks, white parts only

1 medium onion, chopped

4 tablespoons (60g) butter

2 medium potatoes,
    peeled and diced

6 cups (1.5L) Chicken Stock II (page 16)

1 bay leaf

1 cup (250ml) heavy cream

1 tablespoon (10g) chopped fresh
    chives, for garnish

1. Slice the leeks in half lengthwise, rinse well—leeks tend to be gritty—and pat dry. Slice thin, horizontally. Melt the butter in a large saucepan and cook the leeks and onion until soft, about 30 minutes; do not allow to brown.

2. Add the potatoes, chicken stock, and bay leaf. Bring to a boil, reduce the heat, and simmer until the potatoes are soft, about 30 minutes.

3. When the potatoes are done, remove the bay leaf and put the soup through the food mill with a medium disk; you may also purée in a blender and then strain to remove any fibrous bits of the leeks.

4. Stir in the heavy cream. This soup may be served either hot or chilled: if hot, return to the stove and bring just to a simmer and serve immediately; if cold, chill in the refrigerator after adding the cream. Either way, sprinkle with the chives just before serving.

COOKING TIME

1¼ hours

CHILLING TIME

1 to 1½ hours

TEST KITCHEN NOTES

IN SPITE OF ITS NAME, YOU WILL NOT FIND VICHYSSOISE IN ANY FRENCH COOKBOOK, EXCEPT AS AN AMERICAN SPECIALTY. IT WAS CREATED BY CHEF LOUIS DIAT AT NEW YORK'S RITZ HOTEL IN MEMORY OF HIS HOMELAND.

CARROT VICHYSSOISE

INGREDIENTS

2 medium leeks, white parts only

2 tablespoons (30g) butter

2 cups (500ml) Chicken Stock I (page 15)

3 or 4 carrots, diced

1 tablespoon (15ml) lemon juice

Pinch paprika

Salt and freshly ground black pepper,
   to taste

½ cup (125ml) sour cream

Watercress leaves, thin rounds of red or
   green peppers, or chopped cilantro,
   for garnish

1. Halve the leeks lengthwise and rinse them well to remove the grit, then chop them. Cook in the butter in a large saucepan over low heat, about 20 to 30 minutes; do not allow to brown.

2. When the leeks are translucent, add 1 cup (250ml) of the chicken stock and the carrots. Cover and simmer until the carrots are soft, about 20 minutes.

3. Process in a blender until smooth. Add the rest of the chicken stock, the lemon juice, and paprika; adjust the seasoning with salt and pepper. Chill for at least 1½ hours. Just before serving, gradually stir in the sour cream.

4. Serve, garnished with watercress leaves, green or red peppers, or cilantro.

COOKING TIME

45 to 50 minutes

CHILLING TIME

1½ hours

TEST KITCHEN NOTES

WHAT'S WONDERFUL ABOUT THIS VICHYSSOISE VARIATION IS ITS MAGNIFICENT PALE ORANGE COLOR. FOR TANGIER RESULTS, BUTTERMILK MAY BE SUBSTITUTED FOR THE SOUR CREAM.

JERUSALEM ARTICHOKE VICHYSSOISE

SERVES 4

INGREDIENTS

½ cup (125ml) white vinegar

1 pound (500g) Jerusalem artichokes
    (see Test Kitchen Notes)

2 tablespoons (30g) butter

1 medium onion, chopped

1 medium potato, peeled and diced

2 cups (500ml) Chicken Stock I (page 15)

1 to 2 tablespoons (15–30ml) lemon
    juice, to taste

Salt and freshly ground white pepper

1. Mix the vinegar into a large bowl of cold water, then peel the artichokes as close to the water as possible to keep discoloration to a minimum. Keep in the water until ready to use.

2. Heat the butter in a large saucepan over medium heat. Sauté the onion and potato gently in the butter for 5 minutes.

3. As quickly as possible and one at a time, rinse the artichokes, dice them, and stir into the onions and potatoes. Cover and cook over low heat for about 10 minutes, shaking the pan occasionally to prevent sticking.

4. Add the chicken stock and bring to a boil, then reduce the heat and simmer until the vegetables are very tender, about 30 minutes.

5. Purée in a blender in small batches and strain the batches through a wire sieve (to remove any woody bits or lumps) into a large bowl. Add the lemon juice and return soup to the pan to reheat. Adjust the seasoning with salt and white pepper. Serve piping hot.

COOKING TIME

50 minutes

TEST KITCHEN NOTES

THE JERUSALEM ARTICHOKE IS ACTUALLY THE ROOT OF A SUNFLOWER NATIVE TO NORTH AMERICA. IT WAS FIRST INTRODUCED INTO EUROPE BY COLUMBUS, AND IT WAS THE ITALIANS WHO NAMED IT *GIRASOLE* (LITERALLY, "TURN TO THE SUN"). JERUSALEM ARTICHOKES LOOK LIKE A CROSS BETWEEN A POTATO AND GINGER ROOT AND ARE USUALLY YELLOW-BEIGE IN COLOR.

THIS "VICHYSSOISE" IS CLOSE IN CHARACTER TO ITS ORIGINAL POTATO COUSIN, BUT WITH A WONDERFUL TWIST IN ITS FLAVOR THAT NOT EVERYONE WILL RECOGNIZE. IT IS DEFINITELY WORTH ALL THE TROUBLE INVOLVED IN KEEPING THE AIR AWAY FROM THE ARTICHOKES DURING THE PREPARATION PROCESS.

BROCCOLI-CAULIFLOWER SOUP

INGREDIENTS

2 cups (500ml) Chicken Stock II
    (page 16)
½ pound (250g) cauliflower, chopped
1 sprig fresh dill
½ pound (250g) broccoli tops
1 small onion, chopped
2 tablespoons (30g) butter
1 tablespoon (10g) flour
1½ cups (375ml) whole milk
1 cup (125g) grated sharp Cheddar
    cheese
Salt and ground white pepper, to taste
Pinch freshly ground nutmeg

1. Heat 1 cup (250ml) chicken stock in a medium saucepan over medium-high heat. Cook the cauliflower in the chicken stock until soft, about 10 minutes. Transfer to a blender with the dill and purée. Set aside.

2. Coarsely chop the broccoli, setting aside a few of the tiny topmost florets to serve as a garnish (if you like, blanch these before using). Cook the broccoli in the remaining 1 cup (250ml) of broth until bright green, about 5 minutes. Remove from the heat and set aside.

3. Sauté the onion in the butter until tender but not browned, about 10 to 15 minutes. Stir in the flour, then gradually add the milk, stirring constantly. Bring to a simmer and cook 5 minutes; add the cheese, stirring until melted.

4. Just before serving, combine the cauliflower and broccoli mixtures with the milk and cheese. Heat to serving temperature and adjust the seasoning with salt and pepper. Serve hot, garnishing with the reserved broccoli florets and nutmeg.

COOKING TIME

50 minutes

TEST KITCHEN NOTES

THE USE OF FROZEN VEGETABLES WILL CUT THE COOKING TIME OF THIS SOUP IN HALF; BUT YOU WILL ALSO LOSE HALF THE FLAVOR. YOU MAY SUBSTITUTE DRIED DILL FOR THE FRESH, BUT ADD IT WHEN THE CAULIFLOWER IS COOKING. FOR A MORE EXOTIC TWIST, USE ROSEMARY, TARRAGON, OR A PINCH OF CUMIN.

Gazpacho

INGREDIENTS

1½ pounds (750g) tomatoes

2 or 3 sprigs fresh parsley, leaves only

2 sprigs fresh tarragon, leaves only

1 sprig fresh oregano, leaves only

6 fresh basil leaves

2 medium cucumbers, peeled, seeded, and minced fine

1 large green bell pepper, stemmed, seeded, and minced fine

1 medium onion, finely minced

½ cup (125ml) olive oil

Juice of 1 lemon

3 cups (750ml) Chicken Stock I, Chicken Consommé, or Vegetable Broth (page 15, 17, or 20)

Salt and cayenne pepper, to taste

2 tablespoons (30ml) dry sherry

Garlic Croutons (page 11), chopped scallions, and cilantro, for garnish

1. Blanch the tomatoes in boiling water for 2 minutes to facilitate peeling. Peel, core, and seed over a bowl, reserving the juices, then mince fine.

2. Rinse the herbs and mince the leaves very fine. Use your favorite herbs, but use discretion—more is not necessarily better.

3. Stir the tomatoes, herbs, cucumbers, pepper, and onion together in a glass or ceramic bowl. Add the olive oil, lemon juice, reserved tomato juice, and the chicken stock.

4. Adjust the seasoning with salt; add the cayenne judiciously, as it will intensify as the soup chills. Cover and refrigerate to let the flavors blend.

5. After at least 2 or 3 hours, remove the soup and taste; add the sherry at this time. Before serving, garnish with garlic croutons, scallions, and cilantro.

PREPARATION TIME

30 minutes

CHILLING TIME

2 to 3 hours

TEST KITCHEN NOTES

MOST GAZPACHO RECIPES CALL FOR PURÉEING THE VEGETABLES, BUT I PREFER THIS "FINELY CHOPPED" VERSION. AFTER ALL, YOU CAN DRINK A GLASS OF MIXED VEGETABLE JUICE ANY TIME!

CREAM OF TOMATO SOUP

INGREDIENTS

2 tablespoons (30g) butter

1 medium onion, finely minced

1 stalk celery, finely minced

2 tomatoes, seeded and chopped

2 tablespoons (20g) flour

4 cups (1L) cold milk

¼ teaspoon (1.25ml) Worcestershire sauce

Pinch cayenne pepper

Salt and freshly ground black pepper,
     to taste

2 tablespoons (30ml) dry sherry, optional

1. Melt the butter in a large saucepan over medium heat. Cook the onion and celery in the butter for 10 minutes, then stir in the tomatoes. Cover and cook, stirring occasionally, until the tomatoes disintegrate, about 15 minutes.

2. Sprinkle the flour over the tomatoes and cook, stirring, for 5 minutes; gradually add the cold milk and bring to a simmer, continuing to stir constantly. Add the Worcestershire sauce, cayenne, and salt and pepper, and cook for 5 minutes.

3. Put the soup through a sieve to remove skin and any remaining seeds. Add the sherry just before serving.

COOKING TIME

45 minutes

> ### TEST KITCHEN NOTES
>
> VARY THIS SIMPLE SOUP BY THE ADDITION OF YOUR FAVORITE HERBS: BASIL, ROSEMARY, THYME, OR OREGANO COME TO MIND.

POTAGE GERMINY
(Cream of Sorrel Soup)

INGREDIENTS

½ pound (250g) fresh sorrel
     (about 4 cups loosely packed)

2 teaspoons (10g) butter

4 cups (1L) Chicken Stock II (page 16)

Pinch cayenne pepper

Salt and freshly ground black pepper,
     to taste

8 egg yolks

1⅓ cups (333ml) heavy cream

1. Wash the sorrel and shake or pat dry. Remove the stems, including partway up the leaves if they seem tough or stringy. Cut across the leaves in strips.

2. Melt the butter in a medium saucepan. Add the sorrel and wilt it quickly over medium-high heat. Add the stock, cayenne, salt, and pepper and bring to a boil.

3. Beat the egg yolks well with a fork and then beat in the heavy cream. Add a little hot soup to the egg mixture and incorporate, then gradually stir the mixture back into the soup. Cook for 2 minutes, or until the soup coats the back of a spoon; do not let the mixture boil. Serve at once, piping hot. If you must reheat, do it in the top of a double boiler over, but not in, hot water (to avoid scrambling the eggs).

COOKING TIME

10 minutes

> ### TEST KITCHEN NOTES
>
> I PREFER TO SERVE THIS CARDIOLOGIST'S NIGHTMARE HOT, BUT YOU MAY ALSO SERVE IT CHILLED. IF YOU DO, YOU SHOULD ADD AN EXTRA PINCH OF CAYENNE AND LET IT CHILL FOR 1½ HOURS BEFORE SERVING. EITHER WAY, THIS SOUP IS ONE OF THE RICHEST, YET EASIEST TO PREPARE.

CREAM OF FENNEL SOUP

INGREDIENTS

2 fennel bulbs with stalks

3 tablespoons (45g) butter

1 medium onion, diced

1 medium potato, peeled and diced

3 cups (750ml) Vegetable Stock
    (page 20)

½ cup (125ml) whole milk

Salt and ground white pepper, to taste

½ to 1 cup (125–250ml) sour cream

1. Remove the stalks and base of the fennel bulbs, setting aside a few of the feathery tops. Cut the bulbs in quarters lengthwise then slice crosswise into ½-inch (13mm) thick pieces.

2. Melt the butter in a large saucepan over medium-high heat. Sauté the onion in the butter for 3 or 4 minutes, stirring frequently, without browning.

3. Add the potato and diced fennel to the onion. Cook and stir another 5 minutes, until potato and fennel are heated through. Add the stock, bring to a boil, then cover and simmer for 30 minutes, until the vegetables are tender.

4. Purée in a food processor or in a blender in small batches; strain or put through a food mill, then return to the pot. Add the milk and reheat the purée, adjusting the seasoning with salt and pepper. Whisk in the sour cream to taste. Chop the reserved fennel tops. Serve the soup at once, garnishing with the fennel tops.

COOKING TIME

35 to 40 minutes

TEST KITCHEN NOTES

THE FENNEL BULB, THOUGH WIDELY AVAILABLE, IS UNDER-USED AND UNDER-APPRECIATED. ITS SUBTLE ANISE FLAVOR IS SUBDUED IN THIS RECIPE, BUT PLEASANTLY RECALLED TO THE PALATE BY THE TOPS USED AS GARNISH.

CREAM OF MUSHROOM SOUP

INGREDIENTS

⅓ to ½ pound (167–250g) button
    mushrooms

3 tablespoons (45g) butter

2 tablespoons (30g) grated onion

1 tablespoon (10g) all-purpose flour

2 cups (500ml) cold whole milk

¼ cup (125ml) dry sherry, optional

1. Clean and mince the mushrooms. Melt the butter in a large saucepan over medium heat. Gently sauté the mushrooms and onion in the heated butter for 5 minutes, then cover and cook 10 to 15 minutes over low heat.

2. Add the flour and cook, stirring constantly, for a few minutes. Add the cold milk very gradually, stirring constantly to incorporate. Bring the soup to a simmer over medium heat. Reduce the heat to low and cook 20 minutes longer, stirring occasionally. If the heat on your stovetop burner is too high at its lowest, you risk scorching the soup; to prevent this from happening, cook the soup in the top of a double boiler over boiling water for the final 20 minutes.

3. Add the sherry just before serving; reheat just to the simmering point and serve immediately.

COOKING TIME

45 minutes

CREAM OF ASPARAGUS SOUP

INGREDIENTS

½ pound (250g) asparagus

1 tablespoon (15g) butter

¼ cup (45g) shallots, finely minced

2 small inner stalks celery with leaves,
    finely minced

1½ cups (375ml) Chicken Stock II
    (page 16)

½ bay leaf

1 fresh sage leaf, or ⅛ teaspoon
    dried sage

2 egg yolks

1 cup (250ml) heavy cream

Salt and ground white pepper, to taste

1. Rinse the asparagus to remove any grit, then snap off the bottom of each stalk where it breaks easily. Blanch the stalks for 2 or 3 minutes in 4 cups (1L) boiling water. Halt the cooking while the asparagus is still crisp and bright green; drain, reserving the cooking water, and refresh the asparagus quickly in cold water. Cut off the tips and set them aside for garnish; cut the stalks into ½-inch (13mm) pieces.

2. Melt the butter in a large saucepan. Add the shallots and celery and cook over low heat until tender but not browned.

3. Add the asparagus water to the saucepan. Add the chicken stock and the asparagus stalks (but not the tips) along with the bay leaf and sage. Bring to a

boil, then cover and simmer for 20 to 30 minutes, or until the asparagus is very tender. Remove the bay leaf and purée in batches in a blender.

4. Just before serving, reheat the soup to a simmer. While soup is heating, beat the egg yolks in a small bowl, then beat in the heavy cream. Beat a small amount of hot soup into the eggs and cream, then return it all to the pot and, stirring constantly, heat the soup to serving temperature. Add the reserved tips to the pot and adjust the seasoning with salt and ground white pepper to taste.

COOKING TIME

45 minutes

TEST KITCHEN NOTES

ON THE SUBJECT OF SNAPPING OFF VERSUS CUTTING THE BOTTOMS OF THE ASPARAGUS STALKS, I TEND TO BE TRADITIONAL—IF TIME IS NOT AN ISSUE. BY BENDING THE STALK UNTIL IT BREAKS EASILY AND NATURALLY, YOU TEND TO REMOVE THE FIBROUS PORTION WITHOUT WASTING ANY OF THE GOOD CRISP PORTION.

CHINESE ASPARAGUS SOUP I

SERVES 6

INGREDIENTS

12 slender stalks fresh asparagus

5 cups (1.25L) Vegetable Stock (page 20)

Salt and freshly ground black pepper

3 tablespoons (30g) cornstarch

5 tablespoons (75ml) cold water

2 tablespoons (30ml) dry sherry

2 egg whites

1. Rinse the asparagus, snap off the bottoms, and cut the stalks in 1/2-inch (13mm) thick diagonal slices. Toss into boiling water and blanch for 2 or 3 minutes. Remove while still bright green and crisp and rinse in cold water to refresh the asparagus. Set aside.

2. Heat the vegetable stock just to the boiling point. Add the asparagus and bring back to the simmering point; add salt and pepper to taste.

3. Mix the cornstarch with 3 tablespoons (45ml) of the cold water and immediately stir the mixture into the hot broth. Simmer for 1 minute, stir in the sherry, and remove the saucepan from the heat.

4. Beat the egg whites with the remaining 2 tablespoons (30ml) of cold water. Stirring constantly with a circular motion, drizzle the egg white mixture into the steaming broth. The desired effect is to have wisps of white suspended in the broth. Serve immediately.

COOKING TIME

15 minutes

> **TEST KITCHEN NOTES**
>
> IN SPITE OF BEING SERVED PIPING HOT, THIS SOUP IS LIGHT, CRISP, AND REFRESHING, WITH A HINT OF FRESH ASPARAGUS AND A PLEASANT CONTRAST IN TEXTURE BETWEEN THE SLIGHTLY VISCOUS BROTH AND THE JUST BARELY-COOKED VEGETABLE.

CHINESE ASPARAGUS SOUP II

SERVES 3 OR 4

INGREDIENTS

1 can white asparagus
  (12 to 15 ounces [375–450g])

2 cups (500ml) Chicken Stock II (page 16)

Salt, to taste

4 teaspoons (15g) cornstarch

4 tablespoons (60ml) cold water

1 tablespoon (15ml) dry sherry

1 egg white

1. Drain the asparagus, reserving the liquid. Cut the stalks in 1-inch (2.5cm) sections.

2. Heat the chicken stock with the reserved liquid. Add the asparagus and bring to a boil. Add salt to taste.

3. Stir the cornstarch into 3 tablespoons (45ml) of the water, then stir at once into the hot soup. Simmer for 1 minute, add the sherry, and remove the saucepan from the heat.

4. Beat the egg white together with the remaining 1 tablespoon (15ml) of water. Drizzle the mixture into the soup while stirring the soup with a circular motion. Serve immediately.

COOKING TIME

10 minutes

> **TEST KITCHEN NOTES**
>
> THIS SOUP IS DIFFERENT FROM THE ABOVE RECIPE: THE FLAVOR IS MORE INTENSE AND THE APPEARANCE MORE EXOTIC, BUT THE CONTRAST OF TEXTURES IS ABSENT.

BONGO-BONGO SOUP

INGREDIENTS

5 ounces (150g) frozen chopped spinach

2 tablespoons (30g) butter

2 shallots, minced

¼ cup (63ml) dry white wine

1 pound (500g) oysters, shucked, their
   liquor reserved

½ teaspoon salt

Ground white pepper, to taste

3 cups (750ml) Chicken Stock II
   (page 16)

1 cup (250ml) whipping cream

Pinch cayenne

1 teaspoon (5ml) Worcestershire sauce

1 tablespoon (15ml) lemon juice

Sour cream, for garnish

1. Defrost the spinach and drain, thoroughly pressing out all of the liquid. Set aside.

2. Melt the butter in a large saucepan over medium heat and gently cook the shallots until tender but not browned, about 10 minutes. Add the wine, bring to a boil, and cook until the liquid is reduced by half.

3. Add the oysters and their liquor, and the salt and pepper. Warm gently for 2 or 3 minutes, then set aside.

4. In a separate saucepan, bring the chicken stock and the spinach to a boil. Add to the oyster mixture. Transfer to a food processor or a blender and purée.

5. Return the soup to the saucepan and add the cream, cayenne, Worcestershire sauce, and lemon juice. Adjust the salt if necessary. Reheat until piping hot, but do not boil.

6. Serve with sour cream handed around separately.

COOKING TIME

45 minutes

TEST KITCHEN NOTES

THIS RECIPE, MUCH ADAPTED FROM ITS PLAZA HOTEL (NEW YORK) ORIGINS, HAS BEEN KNOWN TO SPOIL GUESTS' APPETITES FOR THE REST OF THEIR DINNER AS THEY REQUEST SECONDS, THEN THIRDS. ITS EMERALD HUE AND CREAMY RICHNESS BELIE ITS SHELLFISH BASE, MAKING IT AN INTRIGUING AND TASTY OPENER.

LOBSTER BISQUE

INGREDIENTS

4 tablespoons (60g) butter

1 carrot, peeled and chopped fine

1 stalk celery, chopped fine

1 small onion, chopped fine

1 medium lobster, about 1½ pounds
    (750g), cooked

4 cups (1L) Fish Fumet (page 21)

2 cups (500ml) dry white wine

2 cups (300g) cooked white rice

1 bay leaf

Salt and ground white pepper, to taste

½ cup (125ml) cognac

1 tablespoon (15g) tomato paste

1 cup (250ml) heavy cream

Pinch cayenne pepper

1. Melt half of the butter in a skillet over low heat. Add the carrot, celery, and onion; cook, covered, until tender but not browned, about 20 minutes.

2. Shell the lobster, reserving the tail and claw meat, and any other significantly sized bits. Toss the shells in the food processor and process as fine as possible, or pulverize in a mortar.

3. Bring the fumet to a simmer in a saucepan. Cook the lobster shells in the fumet for 15 minutes, then strain through a muslin cloth or several layers of cheesecloth to remove any grit and return it to the saucepan.

4. When the vegetable mixture is cooked, add it to the strained fumet with the wine, rice, bay leaf, salt, and white pepper. Bring to a boil, then simmer for 10 to 15 minutes.

5. Discard the bay leaf. At the end of this cooking, purée the soup in a food processor or blender in batches. Return the strained soup to the pot.

6. Dice the lobster meat and add it to the soup with the cognac, tomato paste, heavy cream, and the remaining 2 tablespoons (30ml) butter. Reheat without allowing the soup to boil. Season to taste with salt and a pinch of cayenne, if necessary.

COOKING TIME

45 minutes

TEST KITCHEN NOTES

THOUGH YOU MAY SUBSTITUTE CHICKEN STOCK, IT REALLY IS PREFERABLE TO USE A FISH FUMET FOR THIS ULTIMATE BISQUE TO EMPHASIZE ITS SEAFOOD NATURE; IN EITHER CASE, THE COOKING OF THE PULVERIZED LOBSTER SHELLS FURTHER INTENSIFIES THE LOBSTER FLAVOR. AS YOU WILL SEE, THE DELICIOUS RESULTS JUSTIFY THESE EXTRA STEPS.

SHRIMP BISQUE

SERVES 4

INGREDIENTS

1 pound (500g) shrimp, small or medium
3 tablespoons (15g) fresh bread crumbs
3 cups (750ml) Fish Fumet (page 21)
3 tablespoons (45ml) butter
1 tablespoon (15ml) lemon juice
 (or good herbed white wine vinegar)
Ground nutmeg, to taste
½ cup (125ml) dry white wine
1 egg yolk
½ cup (125ml) heavy cream
Salt, to taste
Generous pinch cayenne pepper
2 tablespoons (30ml) dry sherry
1 teaspoon (5ml) anchovy paste
 or a dash of Asian fish sauce
1 tablespoon (15g) tomato paste,
 optional
Parsley sprigs, for garnish

1. Measure out in a saucepan enough water to cover the shrimp. Bring the water to a boil, plunge in the shrimp, and blanch just long enough for the shrimp to turn pink. Drain, reserving the liquid. Peel the shrimp. Reserve 4 small shrimp to be used as garnish.

2. Soak the bread crumbs in 1 cup (250ml) of the fumet.

3. Melt 1 tablespoon of the butter in a large saucepan over low heat. Add the shrimp and sauté until heated through. Add the lemon juice, nutmeg, and the bread crumbs with their fumet; continue to cook for 5 minutes longer. Remove from the heat and beat in the remaining 2 tablespoons (30ml) butter.

4. Purée the shrimp mixture in a blender or food processor; return to the saucepan, adding the wine and the remaining fumet. Bring to a boil.

5. Beat the egg yolk lightly with a fork, then beat in the heavy cream. Beat a small amount of the hot soup into the egg yolk and cream mixture, then add the mixture to the saucepan. Heat to serving temperature.

6. Adjust the seasoning with salt, cayenne, sherry, and anchovy paste or fish sauce to intensify the seafood flavor. If you find the color too pale, add a tablespoon of tomato paste to give the soup a slight blush.

7. Garnish with a reserved shrimp and a sprig of parsley for each serving.

COOKING TIME

30 minutes

TEST KITCHEN NOTES

THIS IS A GOOD EXAMPLE OF THE USE OF BREAD CRUMBS AS A THICKENER. HOWEVER, IT IS DIFFICULT TO OBTAIN A SMOOTH RESULT, SO A BEURRE MANIÉ (PAGE 124) MAY BE SUBSTITUTED IF YOU WISH. USE THE ANCHOVY OR FISH SAUCE WITH CARE, AS EITHER ONE CAN OVERWHELM; THE SHRIMP HAVE LESS FLAVOR THAN LOBSTER, AND THE IDEA IS TO ENHANCE, WITHOUT BLANKETING, THE DELICATE RICHNESS OF THIS BISQUE.

CAULIFLOWER-CARAWAY SOUP

INGREDIENTS

1 pound (500g) cauliflower

5 tablespoons (75g) butter

2 onions, chopped

2 teaspoons caraway seeds, ground or
    well-bruised in a mortar or blender

3 cups (750ml) Chicken Stock I (page 15)

2 teaspoons (10ml) lemon juice

Salt and freshly ground black pepper,
    to taste

2 plum tomatoes, for garnish

1 tablespoon (10g) finely chopped fresh
    parsley, for garnish

1. Peel the stems of the cauliflower to avoid stringiness in the purée; slice the cauliflower thin, setting aside 1 cup (250ml) of the florets for garnish. Blanch these florets in boiling water to cover for 3 minutes. Drain, rinse in cold water to refresh, and set aside.

2. Melt 4 tablespoons (60g) of the butter in a saucepan. Add the onions and cook, stirring, over low heat until the onions are soft—do not allow onions to color. Add the caraway seeds, chicken stock, and sliced cauliflower and bring to a boil. Reduce the heat, cover, and simmer, stirring occasionally, until the cauliflower is tender, about 20 minutes.

3. When the cauliflower is tender, purée in batches in a blender. Return to the saucepan. Add the lemon juice, salt, pepper, and the reserved florets.

4. Meanwhile, peel the tomatoes by blanching briefly in boiling water until the skins pop—they will then slip off readily. Quarter lengthwise to remove the seeds, then chop coarsely. Melt the remaining tablespoon (15g) of butter in a small skillet, add the tomatoes and cook for 5 minutes. Season to taste with salt and pepper.

5. Before serving, reheat the soup. If you are serving it from a tureen at the table, sprinkle the chopped parsley and cauliflower florets over the top and hand the tomato garnish around separately. If you are dishing the soup out at the stove, garnish each serving with tomatoes, and parsley as you serve.

COOKING TIME

50 minutes

TEST KITCHEN NOTES

THIS RECIPE COMES FROM A FRIEND IN FRANCE, WHERE EATING SOUP IS STILL A DAILY RITUAL. THE TOMATO GARNISH IS THE PERFECT COUNTERPOINT TO THE CAULIFLOWER, BOTH IN COLOR AND FLAVOR.

CUCUMBER SOUP

INGREDIENTS

2 cucumbers

1 quart (1L) buttermilk

¼ cup parsley leaves, chopped

4 scallions, white parts only,
    coarsely chopped

2 cups (500ml) sour cream

1 teaspoon salt

2 tablespoons (30ml) freshly squeezed
    lemon juice

2 tablespoons fresh dill, or
    1 teaspoon dried

1. Wash one cucumber. Cut 16 very thin slices and set aside for garnish.

2. Peel the cucumbers, slice in half lengthwise, and scoop out and discard the seeds. Chop the remaining flesh and place half in the blender with 1 cup (250ml) of the buttermilk, the parsley leaves, and scallions. (If using dried dill rather than fresh, add it now to allow the flavor to develop.) Blend until smooth, then pour the purée into the tureen.

3. Whisk the remaining buttermilk, sour cream, salt, and lemon juice into the contents of the tureen. Chill thoroughly before serving.

4. To serve, whisk briefly, then float the reserved cucumber slices on top of the soup. Sprinkle the fresh dill wisps over all.

PREPARATION TIME

20 minutes

CHILLING TIME

1½ hours

TEST KITCHEN NOTES

ALTHOUGH SOME CUCUMBER SOUPS USE CHICKEN STOCK INSTEAD OF BUTTERMILK, IT STRIKES ME THAT THIS SOUP, WHICH IS DELIGHTFUL AS A REFRESHER ON THE HOTTEST DAYS OF THE SUMMER, SHOULD BE KEPT VEGETARIAN AND UNCOOKED. IT IS ALSO A DISH WITH AN INTERNATIONAL REACH: MADE WITH THICK YOGURT INSTEAD OF SOUR CREAM AND BUTTERMILK, WITH ADDED CHOPPED WALNUTS, IT BECOMES BULGARIAN; WHEN YOU REPLACE THE LEMON JUICE WITH RED WINE VINEGAR, IT'S TURKISH CACIK; REPLACE THE PARSLEY WITH A TABLESPOON OF CILANTRO AND A TINY PINCH OF CAYENNE, AND THE SOUP SLIPS INTO MEXICO.

COLD CANTALOUPE SOUP

INGREDIENTS

1 cantaloupe, about 2 pounds (1kg)

2 tablespoons (30g) butter

½ cup (125ml) milk

½ cup (125ml) heavy cream

Juice of ½ lemon

Salt and freshly ground black pepper,
    to taste

Pinch curry powder or a grating
    of nutmeg

¼ cup (30g) toasted sliced almonds,
    for garnish

1. Peel, seed, and dice the cantaloupe. You should have about 3 cups (750g).

2. Melt the butter in a saucepan with a lid; add the cantaloupe, cover, and cook over low heat until very tender, about 10 minutes.

3. Press the cantaloupe and its juices through a wire strainer or a food mill, then whisk in the milk and cream (or substitute buttermilk for a lighter soup). Incorporate the lemon juice.

4. Season with a light hand: salt, pepper, and curry or nutmeg.

5. Chill thoroughly for at least 1½ hours; serve garnished with the almonds.

COOKING TIME

10 minutes

CHILLING TIME

1½ to 2 hours

TEST KITCHEN NOTES

THIS IS A FRUIT SOUP FOR THE BEGINNING OF THE MEAL, DESIGNED TO PLEASE THE EYE AS WELL AS TICKLE THE PALATE. IT WILL TRANSFORM YOUR SIMPLEST MEAL INTO A SUMPTUOUS REPAST. USE 1 CUP (250ML) BUTTERMILK INSTEAD OF THE MILK AND CREAM DURING THE VERY HOTTEST DAYS OF THE SUMMER, AND THE MILK-AND-CREAM VERSION FOR COOLER TIMES.

YIN AND YANG SOUP

INGREDIENTS

2 cups (500ml) Chicken Stock I
    (page 15)
1 cup (180g) green peas, fresh or frozen
¾ teaspoon salt
¼ teaspoon sugar
2 tablespoons (30ml) cold water
1 tablespoon (10g) cornstarch
½ pound (250g) cauliflower florets,
    coarsely chopped
Pinch ground cumin

1. Put 1 cup (250ml) of chicken stock in each of two saucepans. In one, place the peas, ½ teaspoon of salt, and the sugar. Cover, bring to a boil, and simmer until tender, about 10 minutes—but don't allow them to lose their bright color. Remove from the heat and purée in a blender, then return to the saucepan. In a small bowl, mix the water with 1 teaspoon of the cornstarch; stir this paste into the pea purée to thicken.

2. While the peas are cooking, put the cauliflower florets in the other saucepan of chicken stock with the remaining ¼ teaspoon of salt and the cumin. Bring to a boil, then simmer until tender, about 8 minutes. Purée the cauliflower mixture in the blender, then return the soup to its saucepan. In a small bowl, mix the remaining water and cornstarch; stir this paste into the cauliflower soup as a thickener.

3. Just before serving, heat both soups to a simmer. Choose the thicker of the two and carefully place it in one half of a warmed soup plate. Tilting the bowl slightly so that the filled side is down, add the other purée alongside the first. Tease the two soups into the classic yin-yang pattern using the backs of two tablespoons or wooden spoons. The visual effect is stunning, but reheating is a challenge; if necessary, the feat can be accomplished in the microwave or over hot water, so choose your soup plates carefully.

COOKING TIME

25 minutes

TEST KITCHEN NOTES

ANY PURÉED SOUPS CAN BE USED FOR THIS PRESENTATION AS LONG AS THE FLAVORS ARE COMPATIBLE AND THE COLORS CONTRAST. TRY BLACK BEAN PURÉE, POTATO, CARROT VICHYSSOISE, TOMATO, CORN...TURN YOUR IMAGINATION LOOSE.

AVOCADO SOUP

SERVES 4

INGREDIENTS

2 medium leeks, white part only

2 tablespoons (30g) butter

1 small onion, chopped

½ teaspoon curry powder

2 medium potatoes,
    peeled and cubed

2 cups (500ml) Chicken Stock II
    (page 16)

Pinch cayenne pepper

1 ripe avocado (see Test Kitchen Notes)

1 cup heavy cream

Salt and freshly ground black pepper,
    to taste

TEST KITCHEN NOTES

THERE ARE TWO VARIETIES OF AVOCADO, THE HAAS, WHICH HAS A THICK BLACK SKIN, AND THE FUERTE, WHICH HAS A THIN GREEN SKIN AND IS A LITTLE MORE BUTTERY IN TASTE AND TEXTURE. EITHER WORKS FINE, BUT WHICHEVER YOU USE IT MUST BE RIPE; TEST FOR THIS BY FEELING THE NECK OF THE AVOCADO, WHICH SHOULD YIELD SLIGHTLY. THE REST OF THE FRUIT SHOULD BE FAIRLY FIRM.

IF THE HEAVY CREAM SEEMS TOO RICH, TRY LIGHT CREAM. BE PRUDENT WITH THE CURRY POWDER AND CAYENNE—THE DELICATE FLAVOR OF AVOCADO NEEDS A SLIGHT BOOST BUT IS EASILY OVERWHELMED.

1. To best rid leeks of the grit, halve lengthwise and rinse. Pat dry and chop. Melt the butter in a large saucepan over medium heat. Add the leeks and onion and cook until tender but not browned, about 10 minutes.

2. Add the curry powder and the potatoes. Cook and stir over low heat for 5 minutes. Add the chicken stock and cayenne. Bring to a boil and simmer until the potatoes are tender, about 15 minutes. Skim if necessary, then allow to cool to room temperature, about 1 hour.

3. Pit and peel the avocado. Put it in the blender with the broth and purée. Add the cream and blend again; adjust the seasoning with salt and pepper. Chill slightly before serving, about 30 minutes; this is one cold soup that should not be icy, but in-between cold.

COOKING TIME

45 minutes

COOLING TIME

1½ hours

WONTON SOUP

INGREDIENTS

¼ pound (125g) pork, diced

¼ pound (125g) shrimp,
    peeled and deveined

2 scallions, diced

1 small, thin slice ginger root

1 teaspoon (5ml) soy sauce

1 small clove garlic, pressed

1 egg, slightly beaten

1 package (about 25) wonton wrappers

6 to 8 cups (1.75–2L) Chicken Stock II
    (page 16)

2 tablespoons (20g) chopped cilantro,
    chives, or scallions, for garnish

1. Process the pork and shrimp together in a blender or food processor until fine.

2. Add and process the scallions, ginger, soy sauce, garlic, and 1 tablespoon (15ml) of the beaten egg. Remove paste from blender or processor and set aside.

3. In the center of each wonton wrapper, place about 1 teaspoon (5ml) of the shrimp-and-pork paste. Fold the wrapper over the filling on the diagonal; lift the ends of the long end of this triangle and press them together, first moistening each point with a little of the beaten egg. This will hold them together. Fold the right angle back in the opposite direction, moistening it also with egg if you don't trust the geometry of the thing to hold it together. Repeat until all the paste is gone; you should get about 24 wontons.

4. Poach the wontons in gently simmering salted water, a few at a time, for about 5 minutes. Remove with a slotted spoon and drain.

5. When all the wontons are cooked, bring to a boil enough chicken stock to allow 1½ cups (375ml) per serving. Simmer the wontons in the broth gently for 1 or 2 minutes to reheat and serve from a tureen, with the garnish of your choice.

COOKING TIME

20 to 25 minutes

TEST KITCHEN NOTES

WONTONS ARE SURPRISINGLY EASY TO MAKE; THE TRICK IS TO DEVELOP A METHOD FOR FOLDING UP THESE DELICIOUS LITTLE DUMPLINGS SO THAT THEY ARE SOUP-PROOF. THEY CAN BE MADE IN ADVANCE, SINCE REWARMING IS A PART OF THE RECIPE.

DOROTHY'S HOLIDAY CONSOMMÉ

SERVES 6

INGREDIENTS

1 dozen Brazil nuts

5½ cups (1.38L) Beef Consommé (page
    19) or 2 10.5-ounce (450ml) cans,
    diluted with water to make 5½ cups
    (1.38L)

¼ cup (63ml) dry sherry or Madeira wine

½ cup (125ml) heavy cream,
    whipped stiff

1. Preheat the oven to 375° F (190°C).

2. Shell the Brazil nuts, then shave the nut meats on the slicer blade of a grater.

Spread the nut meats on a baking sheet and toast until golden in the oven, about 12 minutes. Check occasionally on their progress; they burn easily.

3. Bring the consommé to a simmer. Just before serving, add the sherry or Madeira wine. Do not allow to boil again, but serve piping hot with the Brazil nuts and whipped cream handed around separately.

COOKING TIME

15 to 20 minutes

TEST KITCHEN NOTES

THIS SOUP APPEARS ON OUR HOLIDAY TABLE TWICE EVERY YEAR. IN FACT, MY FAMILY COULDN'T PROCEED IN THE YULETIDE MOOD IF ONE OF THE CHILDREN WEREN'T POPPING SHELLS ALL OVER THE KITCHEN AND I DIDN'T BURN AT LEAST ONE BATCH OF THE SHAVED NUTS. INCIDENTALLY, EVEN CANNED CONSOMMÉ IS DELICIOUS AND FESTIVE WHEN PRESENTED THIS WAY.

CONSOMMÉ WITH DIABLOTINS

SERVES 5

INGREDIENTS

20 ½-inch (13mm) thick rounds
    French baguette

2 tablespoons (30g) butter

2 tablespoons (20g) flour

1 cup (250ml) cold milk

¼ teaspoon cayenne, or to taste

⅓ cup (63g) grated Parmesan cheese

Salt, to taste

5 cups (1.25L) Chicken Consommé
    (page 17)

1. Preheat the oven to 400° F (200°C).

2. Put the rounds of French bread on a baking sheet and toast very lightly in the oven, about 5 minutes. Check occasionally to prevent over-toasting.

3. Melt the butter in a saucepan over medium heat. Stir in the flour until there are no lumps. Continue to cook and stir 1 minute longer, then gradually add the milk, stirring constantly to avoid lumps. Add the cayenne, lower the heat, and cook for 5 minutes. Stir in the Parmesan. Add salt to taste.

4. Heat the consommé and transfer to a tureen, from which to serve.

5. Make smooth rounded domes of the Parmesan paste on the slices of toast. Brown lightly under the broiler and serve as a side dish.

COOKING TIME

30 minutes

TEST KITCHEN NOTES

THE NAME "DIABLOTIN," OR "LITTLE DEVIL," IS A TRIBUTE TO THE TOAST'S CAYENNE CONTENT.

CONSOMMÉ BRUNOISE

INGREDIENTS

3 tablespoons (45g) butter

2 medium carrots, peeled and diced fine

2 turnips, peeled and diced fine

½ bunch celery, diced fine

1 large leek, white part only, thoroughly
　　cleaned and diced fine

Salt, to taste

Pinch sugar

5 cups (1.25L) Beef Consommé
　　(page 19)

Chopped chervil or parsley, for garnish

1. Melt the butter in a heavy-bottomed saucepan over medium heat; add the carrots, turnips, celery, and leek; cover

and cook very gently for about 25 minutes without browning. Shake the pan or stir occasionally to avoid scorching. When the vegetables are tender, add the salt and sugar.

2. Add the consommé; bring to a boil and simmer for 10 minutes. Skim if necessary.

3. Serve with a sprinkling of chopped chervil, if available, or parsley.

COOKING TIME

35 minutes

> **TEST KITCHEN NOTES**
>
> THIS IS A FAIRLY HEARTY VEGETABLE SOUP, THOUGH IT RETAINS A CONSOMMÉ FLAVOR. IT CAN BE MADE INTO A MEAL BY THE ADDITION OF A FEW QUENELLES (PAGE 12), OR BY GARNISHING IT WITH DIABLOTINS (SEE CONSOMMÉ WITH DIABLOTINS, PAGE 105) OR CREAM CHEESE TARTLETS (PAGE 13).

CONSOMMÉ COLBERT

INGREDIENTS

1 large carrot, diced

½ cup (90g) peeled and diced turnip

½ cup (90g) diced green beans

½ cup (90g) green peas

5 cups (1.25L) Chicken Consommé
　　(page 17)

4 cups (1L) water

Vegetable bouillon cube

5 small eggs

1. Bring a large pot of salted water to a boil. Add the carrot, turnip, and green

beans and cook for 15 minutes. Drain the vegetables and refresh them under cold water.

2. In a saucepan, combine the carrot, turnip, green beans, the green peas, and consommé. Bring to a boil and cook for 10 minutes.

3. Bring the water to a boil in a skillet. Add the bouillon cube and stir until dissolved. Add the eggs and poach until the whites are completely opaque, about 2½ minutes. Serve the consommé in

soup plates with a few of the vegetables and one poached egg per serving.

COOKING TIME

30 minutes

> **TEST KITCHEN NOTES**
>
> FOR EXPEDIENCY'S SAKE, YOU MAY USE ALL FROZEN VEGETABLES, THOUGH THEY ARE LESS FLAVORFUL THAN THE FRESH ONES. THE POACHED EGG MAKES THIS A SURPRISINGLY FILLING SOUP.

CONSOMMÉ AURORA

INGREDIENTS

5 cups (1.25L) Beef Consommé (page
    19) or 2 10.5-ounce (450ml) cans,
    diluted with water to make 5 cups
    (1.25L)
2 tablespoons (20g) tapioca
2 ounces (60g) chicken breast,
    julienned quite thin
¼ cup (60g) tomato paste

1. Bring the consommé to a boil.
Sprinkle in the tapioca, stirring constantly.
Lower the heat and simmer the soup
about 5 minutes, stirring occasionally.

2. Add the chicken to the consommé
and cook for 2 minutes.

3. Put the tomato paste in a small
bowl. Dilute with ½ cup (125ml) of the
hot consommé, then return the mixture
to the saucepan. Return to a simmer
before serving.

COOKING TIME

15 minutes

TEST KITCHEN NOTES

THIS IS DEFINITELY A CONSOMMÉ WITH
A BLUSH, HENCE ITS NAME. THE USE OF
TAPIOCA AS A THICKENER ENSURES THAT
THE SOUP RETAINS SOME CLARITY WHILE
PROVIDING SOME BODY FOR THE JULIENNED
CHICKEN.

FLORENTINE CONSOMMÉ

INGREDIENTS

5 cups (1.25L) Chicken Consommé
    (page 17) or Chicken Stock II
    (page 16)
15 medium-sized spinach leaves
    or 1 or 2 tablespoons frozen
    whole-leaf spinach, thawed,
    cut cross-wise into thin strips
¼ cup (20g) cooked rice
2 eggs, thoroughly beaten
1 loaf of crusty bread

1. Bring the consommé to a boil.
Toss in the spinach leaves and crumble
in the rice using your fingers to make
sure the grains are separated.

2. Stir the soup with a circular motion
and begin drizzling in the eggs so that
long filaments of egg form in the simmering liquid. If there is an extra pair of
hands available, have them drizzle the
eggs through a strainer while you stir.

3. Serve piping hot, with thick slices
of crusty bread on the side.

COOKING TIME

5 minutes

TEST KITCHEN NOTES

IF YOU SUBSTITUTE CHICKEN STOCK FOR
THE CONSOMMÉ AND LEAVE OUT THE
SPINACH AND RICE YOU WILL FIND YOU
HAVE A CLASSIC EGG-DROP SOUP, WHICH
MAY BE SERVED PLAIN OR GARNISHED WITH
A SPRINKLING OF FINELY CHOPPED CHIVES
OR SCALLIONS.

ARMENIAN MONTI IN BROTH

SERVES 8

INGREDIENTS

FOR THE YOGURT SAUCE

1 cup (227g) plain yogurt
1 clove garlic, pressed
2 tablespoons (20g) finely minced parsley
Pinch salt

FOR THE PASTRY

1 egg
3 tablespoons (45ml) water
½ teaspoon salt
2 tablespoons (30g) butter, melted
    and cooled
1½ cups (170g) all-purpose flour

FOR THE FILLING

½ pound (250g) ground lamb
1 small onion, minced fine
1 clove garlic, minced fine
2 tablespoons (20g) minced parsley
½ teaspoon salt
Freshly ground pepper, to taste

1 egg white, lightly beaten with a fork

FOR THE BROTH

8 cups (2L) Beef Stock or Consommé
    (page 18 or 19)
4 teaspoons (20g) tomato paste
Pinch cayenne

1. Combine the yogurt sauce ingredients in a bowl. Cover and refrigerate for at least 1 hour to allow the flavors to develop and blend.

2. To make the pastry dough: In a bowl, combine the egg, water, salt, and butter. Gradually add the flour until the dough forms a ball. Turn it out on a floured surface and knead until the dough is smooth and elastic, adding additional flour as necessary to avoid sticking. Cover and let rest for 30 minutes.

3. While the dough is resting, make the filling: Thoroughly combine the lamb, onion, garlic, parsley, salt, and pepper in a bowl. Set aside to let the flavors develop.

4. Divide the dough in half; roll it out one-half at a time into 9-inch (23cm) squares about ⅛ inch (3mm) thick; cut each half into 1½-inch (4cm) squares, or 72 in all.

5. Preheat the oven to 375°F (190°C). Generously butter a baking dish.

6. Place a ½ teaspoon filling on each pastry square (the meat will shrink during the baking process). Brush two opposite sides with the egg white, then fold the square up into a sort of tiny, flat-bottomed canoe with a very small opening, pressing the sides together. Be sure to fold up the egg-washed sides, since the wash will help the dough stick together. Place the filled Monti in the baking dish as you finish them.

7. Bake until crisp and golden, about 15 minutes. Remove from oven and let cool while you prepare the broth.

8. Combine the stock, tomato paste, and cayenne in a wide saucepan. Bring to a boil. Adjust the seasoning if necessary.

9. Ladle piping hot broth into soup plates, floating 3 to 8 monti (depending on what course the soup is) in each. Hand the yogurt sauce around separately.

PREPARATION TIME

2 hours

COOKING TIME

25 minutes

TEST KITCHEN NOTES

THESE PASTIES DIFFER FROM MOST THAT ARE SERVED IN SOUPS IN THAT THEY ARE BAKED, THEN FLOATED IN BROTH. TO MAKE THE PREPARATION A BREEZE, START EARLY: MONTI MAY BE STORED REFRIGERATED UP TO 2 DAYS, OR FROZEN FOR LONGER PERIODS.

SIBERIAN PEL'MENI SOUP

INGREDIENTS

FOR THE PASTA

2 cups (280g) all-purpose flour
1 egg, beaten lightly with a fork
½ teaspoon salt
3 tablespoons (45ml) water

FOR THE FILLING

1 small onion, minced very fine
6 ounces (175g) finely ground beef
6 ounces (175g) finely ground pork
1 tablespoon (15ml) cold water
½ teaspoon salt
Freshly ground black pepper, to taste
¼ teaspoon cinnamon

6 to 8 cups (1.75–2L) Beef or Chicken
    Stock (page 18 or 16)
Sour cream, for garnish

1. To make the pasta dough: Make a mound of the flour in a broad bowl, making a well in the center of the mound to receive the egg, salt, and water. Working outwards from the central well, gradually incorporate the dry ingredients into the wet. If necessary, you may adjust wet and dry ingredients as needed. When the dough is stiff, move it to a floured surface and knead it briefly, then let it rest in the bowl, covered, for 30 minutes.

2. Roll out quite thin and cut out 48 small circles—about 2½ inches (6.3cm) in diameter—using a biscuit or doughnut cutter (without its "hole") or small wine glass.

3. To make the filling: Combine the onion with the beef, pork, water, salt, pepper, and cinnamon. Mix thoroughly.

4. Place about ½ teaspoon of filling on each circle of pasta, moisten the rim, fold it in half, and press the edges together using your fingers or a fork. Do not overfill the Pel'meni—leave a little room so that juices may spread inside. Lay the completed pasties out on a floured board in a single layer as you work.

5. Bring the stock to a boil. Drop the Pel'meni a few at a time into the stock and simmer about 10 minutes; as soon as they float to the top, scoop them out using a slotted spoon. Keep them in a single layer until all are cooked. For a starter soup you will need about 6 Pel'meni per serving; for a main dish, about 10. When you are ready to serve, reheat the Pel'meni briefly in the stock and serve with sour cream on the side.

PREPARATION TIME

2 hours

COOKING TIME

30 minutes

TEST KITCHEN NOTES

THESE DELICIOUS LITTLE PASTIES CAN BE MADE IN ADVANCE AND STORED IN THE REFRIGERATOR FOR TWO DAYS—ALWAYS IN SINGLE LAYERS OR SEPARATED BY PLASTIC WRAP. ANY PASTIES NOT NEEDED IMMEDIATELY MAY BE SIMMERED IN SALTED WATER FOR ABOUT 10 MINUTES, DRAINED, AND FROZEN FOR LATER USE. BE CAREFUL TO FREEZE THEM INITIALLY IN SINGLE LAYERS; ONCE FROZEN THEY MAY BE STORED IN BAGS OR OTHER CONTAINERS. I UNDERSTAND THAT ORGANIZED SIBERIAN HOUSEWIVES KEEP HUNDREDS OF PEL'MENI IN THEIR COLD CELLARS IN CASE OF VISITORS (EXPECTED OR OTHERWISE).

IN ADDITION TO THEIR USE IN SOUP, PEL'MENI, ONCE BOILED, MAY BE FRIED GENTLY IN BUTTER AND SERVED WITH SOUR CREAM AND PICKLED BEETS AS A SORT OF SIBERIAN PASTA DISH.

DESSERT SOUPS

The new kid on the block in the world of soups is the dessert soup. It is usually fruit-based, served cold, and of a consistency somewhere between a pudding and a fruit salad. A fruit soup can be as sweet as you wish it to be, but is at its best when the fruit is allowed to speak for itself. As a finale to a summer meal (and in some cases during other seasons, too), there is nothing more deliciously refreshing than a fresh fruit soup with (or without) a hint of wine and spices and just a touch of sweetness.

APRICOT SOUP

SERVES 4

INGREDIENTS

1 pound (500g) apricots

3 cups (750ml) water

1 tablespoon quick-cooking tapioca

5 tablespoons (75g) sugar

Grated nutmeg, for garnish

Mint leaves, for garnish

½ cup (114g) yogurt, optional

1. Wash, stone, and coarsely chop the apricots, cutting out any bruises or bad spots. Put in a saucepan with the water, bring to a boil and cook 5 to 10 minutes, depending on the ripeness of the fruit, until disintegrated. Strain through a sieve or food mill. Set aside.

2. Mix the tapioca and sugar in a bowl, add a little of the hot soup, incorporate, then return it all to the saucepan. Bring to a boil, remove from the heat, and let cool for a few minutes. Cover and refrigerate for 1 to 2 hours to thoroughly chill.

3. Serve cold with a light grating of nutmeg, a mint leaf or two per bowl, and a dollop of plain yogurt.

COOKING TIME

20 minutes

CHILLING TIME

1 to 2 hours

> **TEST KITCHEN NOTES**
>
> THIS SOUP CAME TO US WITH A RECOMMENDED GARNISH OF SOUR CREAM, BUT EVEN THE YOGURT SEEMS ALMOST SUPERFLUOUS TO ITS SNAPPY FRESHNESS. A TRULY DELIGHTFUL (AND BEAUTIFUL) AFTER-DINNER TREAT FOR ALL ITS SIMPLICITY, THIS SOUP MAY ALSO BE MADE WITH PEACHES, USING SLIGHTLY LESS SUGAR (TO TASTE) AND A TABLESPOON OF LEMON JUICE.

RASPBERRY-WINE SOUP

INGREDIENTS

12 ounces (375g) raspberries

¾ cup (150g) packed brown sugar

1 cup (250ml) dry rosé wine

1 cup (250ml) fat-free buttermilk

⅛ teaspoon vanilla extract

1 kiwi fruit, peeled and sliced thin, and
    whole mint leaves, for garnish

1. Rinse and pick over the raspberries. Place the raspberries, brown sugar, wine, buttermilk, and vanilla in a blender and process until smooth.

2. Using the back of a spoon, press the puree through a strainer to remove the seeds. Chill thoroughly before serving, at least 1 to 2 hours.

3. Serve in sherbet glasses, garnished with kiwi slices and a few mint leaves.

PREPARATION TIME

10 minutes

CHILLING TIME

1 to 1½ hours

TEST KITCHEN NOTES

DO NOT NEGLECT THE STRAINING OF THE SOUP: THE SEEDS ARE HIGHLY OBTRUSIVE AND DETRACT FROM BOTH THE APPEARANCE AND TEXTURE OF THIS OTHERWISE FABULOUS BUT SIMPLE DESSERT.

STRAWBERRY SOUP

SERVES 4

INGREDIENTS

2 cups (500ml) water
½ cup (95g) sugar
1 quart (1kg) strawberries
½ cup (125ml) sour cream, for garnish

1. Bring 1 cup (250ml) of water to a boil. Add the sugar and stir to make a simple syrup, about 8 minutes. Remove from the heat and add the second cup of water to hasten the cooling process.

2. Wash and hull the strawberries, setting aside a few of the best-looking ones to chop and use as garnish.

3. Process the berries in batches in a blender with the sugar syrup, then strain.

4. Chill thoroughly, at least 1½ hours. Serve, garnished with the reserved chopped berries and a dollop of sour cream.

COOKING TIME

5 minutes

CHILLING TIME

1½ to 2 hours

TEST KITCHEN NOTES

THIS RECIPE MAY ALSO BE MADE WITH MIXED BERRIES (RASPBERRIES AND BLACK-BERRIES ARE GOOD ADDITIONS).

STRAWBERRY CREAM SOUP

SERVES 4 OR 5

INGREDIENTS

1 quart (1kg) strawberries
1 cup (250ml) orange juice
Pinch allspice
Pinch cinnamon
4 teaspoons (15g) instant tapioca
1 cup (250ml) buttermilk
2 tablespoons (30ml) freshly squeezed
    lemon juice, or to taste
8 or 10 mint leaves, for garnish

1. Wash and hull the strawberries; set aside a few of the nicest-looking berries for garnish.

2. Place the remaining berries in a blender with the orange juice, allspice, and cinnamon. Purée until smooth, then strain into a saucepan.

3. Put the tapioca into a small bowl; stir in a small amount of the purée. Return the mixture to the saucepan. Bring to a boil, stirring constantly; lower the heat and continue to cook, stirring, for 1 minute.

4. When the soup begins to thicken, remove the saucepan from the heat and add the buttermilk, then lemon juice to taste. Chill thoroughly in the refrigerator, at least for 1½ hours.

5. Slice the reserved berries and garnish each serving with a few berry slices and mint leaves.

COOKING TIME

5 minutes

CHILLING TIME

1½ to 2 hours

TEST KITCHEN NOTES

THIS COMPLEX SOUP HAS THE AIR OF A PUDDING, BUT NO SUGAR; THE LOOK OF ICE CREAM BUT THE CLEAN FEEL OF A CHILLED FRUIT DRINK ON A HOT DAY.

PUMPKIN SOUP

INGREDIENTS

FOR THE SOUP

2 cups (550g) canned pumpkin purée

½ cup (125ml) whole milk

⅛ teaspoon grated nutmeg

⅛ teaspoon ground cloves

⅛ teaspoon ground ginger

½ teaspoon cinnamon

⅓ cup (75g) packed brown sugar

1 egg yolk

¼ cup (63ml) heavy cream

2 tablespoons (30ml) dark rum

FOR THE GARNISH

½ cup (60g) broken pecan meats

1 tablespoon (15g) melted butter

½ teaspoon granulated sugar

1 tablespoon (15ml) dark molasses

½ cup (125ml) heavy cream, whipped

1. Put the pumpkin purée into a saucepan with the milk, spices, and brown sugar. Bring to a simmer and cook 5 to 10 minutes, stirring occasionally.

2. Using a fork, beat the egg yolk vigorously in a small bowl, then beat in the heavy cream. Stir a little of the pumpkin mixture into the egg mixture and whisk to incorporate, then return it all to the saucepan. Gently heat to just below the simmering point, flavor with the dark rum, then remove from the heat and allow to cool partially.

3. Preheat the oven to 300°F (150°C). Toss the pecans with the butter and granulated sugar. Spread in a single layer on a baking sheet and toast in the oven for about 10 minutes, shaking the pan every 2 minutes to ensure even toasting.

4. To serve, the soup should be barely warm. Drizzle each serving with a little dark molasses and top each one with a couple of spoonsful of whipped cream. Hand the toasted pecans around separately.

COOKING TIME

25 minutes

TEST KITCHEN NOTES

MOST PUMPKIN SOUPS ARE HORS D'OEUVRES; THIS ONE IS AN EXCELLENT FALL DESSERT SOUP THAT HINTS OF THANKSGIVING AND PUMPKIN PIE. THE PURÉE AND NUTS CAN BE PREPARED IN ADVANCE, MAKING THE SOUP ITSELF QUICK AND EASY TO FINISH. IT IS ONE OF THE EXCEPTIONS TO THE COLD OR PIPING-HOT RULE OF SOUP SERVICE, BEING AT ITS BEST WHEN BARELY WARM.

HONEYDEW-CITRUS SOUP

SERVES 4

INGREDIENTS

1 honeydew melon, as ripe as possible

1 tablespoon (15g) unsalted butter

1 grapefruit

1 cup (227g) plain yogurt

About 2 tablespoons (30ml) honey
(or more to taste, and dependent
entirely upon the tartness of the
grapefruit)

½ lime or kiwi fruit, peeled and sliced
thin, for garnish

1. Remove the seeds and rind from the melon and dice the flesh. Melt the butter in a saucepan and add the melon.

Cook briefly, until the melon releases its juices, then cover and cook over medium-low heat for 10 to 15 minutes, stirring occasionally.

2. Purée in a blender or food processor. You should have about 1½ cups (375ml) of purée. Allow to cool about 15 minutes before proceeding.

3. Halve the grapefruit horizontally. Remove the segments, using a knife to free them from the rind and a spoon to transfer them to a bowl; then squeeze out any juice remaining in the halves.

When the honeydew purée is cooled, stir in the grapefruit juice and segments and the yogurt. Process until smooth, then add honey to taste.

4. Chill thoroughly before serving, at least 1½ hours. Garnish each serving with very thin slices of lime or peeled kiwi.

COOKING TIME

20 to 25 minutes

CHILLING TIME

1½ hours

CHILLED PORT-PLUM SOUP

SERVES 4

INGREDIENTS

1 pound (500g) red plums

½ cup (125ml) water

1 cup (250ml) ruby port

⅛ teaspoon cinnamon

¼ cup (48g) sugar

½ cup (125ml) heavy cream

Mint leaves, for garnish

1. Blanch the plums briefly in boiling water; remove them when the skins begin to burst. Discard the used water; peel the plums then return the skins to

the saucepan with the ½ cup (125ml) of water. Bring to a boil and cook for a few minutes to extract what color and flavor you can, then strain the liquid into a small bowl and set aside.

2. Cut the plums in half and remove the pits. Place the flesh in the saucepan with the port, cinnamon, and the reserved plum water. Bring to a boil, reduce the heat, and simmer until the plums are very soft, about 10 minutes.

3. Put the contents of the saucepan in a blender or food processor with the sugar and heavy cream. Blend until smooth. Chill thoroughly, at least 1 to 2 hours. Serve with a garnish of mint leaves.

COOKING TIME

20 minutes

CHILLING TIME

1 to 2 hours

APPLE-CRANBERRY SOUP

SERVES 4

INGREDIENTS

1 pound (500g) cranberries

4 cups (1L) boiling water

Cinnamon stick

1 clove

¾ cup (143g) sugar

½-inch (13mm) × 2-inch (5cm) strip
  orange zest

1½ pounds (750g) tart apples,
  peeled, cored, and thinly sliced

1 tablespoon (10g) cornstarch

1 cup (250ml) cold water

¼ cup (65ml) heavy cream, whipped,
  for garnish

1. Sort and wash the cranberries, then crush them in a saucepan with a wooden mallet. Alternately, coarsely chop by hand or in a food prcessor; add the berries to the saucepan before the next step. Pour the boiling water over the cranberries, then cover the pan and let it stand for 15 minutes off the heat.

2. Strain the juice from the berries and return it to the saucepan. Discard the berries. Stir the cinnamon, clove, sugar, and the orange zest into the juice. Heat the juice over medium-high heat.

3. When the juice boils, add the apples and return to a boil.

4. Dissolve the cornstarch in the cold water. Add this mixture to the soup, stirring until it dissolves. Bring the soup to a simmer and remove it from the heat to cool. Cover and chill in the refrigerator for at least 1½ hours.

5. Serve with whipped cream, sweetened or not, to taste.

COOKING TIME

20 to 25 minutes

CHILLING TIME

1½ to 2 hours

TEST KITCHEN NOTES

ALTHOUGH CHILLING IS THE PRESCRIBED METHOD FOR THIS AUTUMNAL SOUP, I ALSO LIKE IT WARM WITH A SPOONFUL OF VANILLA ICE CREAM. IT SEEMS MORE APPROPRIATE TO THE SEASON THAT WAY. IF YOU CANNOT FIND FRESH CRANBERRIES, YOU MAY SUBSTITUTE 1 QUART (1L) UNSWEETENED CRANBERRY JUICE. IF THIS IS UNAVAILABLE, USE SWEETENED CRANBERRY JUICE BUT ELIMINATE THE SUGAR.

FLOATING ISLAND

INGREDIENTS

4 eggs, separated

1¼ cups (238g) sugar

3¼ cups (813ml) milk

1 teaspoon (5ml) vanilla extract or
    1 tablespoon (15ml) dark rum

Grated nutmeg, to taste

1. Beat the egg whites until quite stiff, then gradually, a tablespoonful at a time, beat in ½ cup (95g) of the sugar.

2. Combine the milk and vanilla in a large saucepan and bring to a boil, then reduce the heat and keep the milk mixture simmering. Float scoops of the egg whites on the hot milk a few at a time so as not to crowd them; you should get about 10 total. Poach for about 3 minutes; then, using a slotted spoon, carefully turn them over. When firm, remove these "islands" from the milk to drain on a clean cloth.

3. To make the custard, beat the egg yolks thoroughly with the remaining sugar. Beating constantly, very gradually add the hot milk to the eggs; then return the mixture to the saucepan. Continue to cook over low heat, stirring constantly, until the custard coats the back of a spoon. Never let the custard boil—if you do, it will separate immediately.

4. Pour the custard into a shallow serving bowl and float the "islands" on it. Sprinkle with a light grating of nutmeg. Chill thoroughly before serving, at least 1 hour.

COOKING TIME

15 to 20 minutes

CHILLING TIME

1 hour

TEST KITCHEN NOTES

THIS IS TRULY A QUICK DESSERT, BUT IT REQUIRES CONSTANT ATTENTION FOR THE BRIEF PERIOD OF ITS COOKING, IN ORDER TO AVOID SCRAMBLING THE EGGS. I HAD OFTEN WONDERED HOW TO CLASSIFY THIS DELICIOUS, LIGHT, CLASSIC DESSERT. THE ADVENT OF DESSERT SOUPS SOLVED THE QUANDARY, FOR OBVIOUSLY FLOATING ISLAND IS A SOUP. THE CUSTARD REMAINS LIQUID AND THE TENDER, AIRY ISLANDS REQUIRE NO KNIFE OR FORK TO CUT THEM.

MIXED FRUIT SOUP

INGREDIENTS

2 cups (500ml) dry rosé wine

½ cup (95g) + 1 tablespoon (15g) sugar

2 or 3 sprigs of rosemary, spearmint, or
    peppermint

2 pounds (1kg) fruit of at least four
    different kinds (strawberries,
    cherries, apricots, peaches,
    raspberries, blackberries, currants,
    melon, pears, and so on)

1 cup (227g) plain yogurt

1. Pour the wine into a saucepan and heat until steaming but not boiling. Remove from the heat; stir in ½ cup (95g) of the sugar until dissolved.

2. Rub the herb sprigs between the palms of your hands to bruise and release the flavor. Place the herbs in the wine syrup and let steep 5 minutes while you prepare the fruit.

3. Wash and prepare all of the fruit. Cut cherries in half and remove the pits, slice and stone apricots, peel and thinly slice peaches. If strawberries are under-ripe, slice and add now (otherwise, to prevent further wilting they should be added just before serving along with other such fragile fruits as raspberries, blackberries, bananas, and so on).

4. When the fruit is prepared, place the sturdier varieties in a nonreactive bowl. Remove the herbs from the syrup and discard them; pour the syrup over the fruit. Let stand, covered, at least 1 hour to allow the flavors to develop.

5. Whip the remaining 1 tablespoon of sugar into the yogurt; set aside for garnish.

6. When ready to serve, add the soft or fragile fruits to the bowl and combine gently to avoid bruising. Ladle the soup into individual bowls, topping each one with a dollop of sweetened yogurt.

COOKING TIME

5 minutes

STEEPING TIME

1 hour

TEST KITCHEN NOTES

THIS IS AN EXCELLENT USE FOR LESS-THAN-PERFECT FRUIT OF THE SEASON. IT DIFFERS FROM A FRUIT SALAD IN THE COMPOSITION, COOKING, AND ABUNDANCE OF ITS FRUIT SYRUP. LIKE OTHER FRUIT SOUPS, IT TOPS OFF A SUMMER MEAL PERFECTLY.

Techniques Et Cetera

EQUIPMENT

Most of the equipment for soup-making is likely to be found in any home kitchen: sauté pans; heavy-bottomed saucepans and pots with well-fitted lids (perfect for long, slow simmering); a good set of knives and a cutting board; a garlic press; and a slotted spoon for skimming. One other small gadget may come in handy, too: an oleophilic brush (a floppy brush made of fibers with a strong affinity for fats), which is a great tool for skimming the residue of fat from the surface of stocks and clear soups.

Of course, you will need the usual measuring cups and spoons, but I cannot stress enough the usefulness of an accurate kitchen scale when dealing with chopped, diced, and sliced ingredients. It is a simple matter to measure out exactly a half pound of tomatoes, for example, and then dice or purée them, but "one medium tomato" is quite another matter. Is it a beefsteak, or a plum tomato? How many plums make one medium beefsteak? Volumetric measurements of chopped solids simply lack precision. Admittedly, in soup-making there is ample room for trial and error, which is one of its beauties, but your kitchen scale will serve you well no matter what you are cooking.

A blender or food processor will speed the mincing and puréeing of both raw and cooked ingredients. Be advised, however, that hot soup in a blender tends to be explosive and should always be puréed in small batches. Use the knob in the lid to periodically release heat and pressure from the blender. The only real restrictions on the food processor have to do with the size of the bowl, but the truth is that they sometimes leak; they are, after all, designed to chop solid foods.

An old-fashioned food mill with interchangeable disks can also be helpful in processing raw and cooked materials. French-style food mills are also available in both stainless steel and plastic; they are used for puréeing cooked foods, but are only marginally less expensive than a blender. They have the advantage of straining out such matter as seeds, peels, and stringy parts, without puréeing them into the soup. Ideally, the food mill should have three changeable disks to allow for degrees of coarseness to your purée.

A variety of gadgets may be used to strain soups: the aforementioned food mill; metal sieves with fine or coarse mesh; nylon sieves; and metal colanders. You're in luck if you happen to have inherited your grandmother's applesauce strainer—the tall inverted conical one on three legs, with a fitted wooden pestle for mashing down cooked fruit. It is ideal for removing the skins and seeds from cooked tomatoes. For the straining of very fine particles, you may line a metal sieve or colander with a clean, damp cloth of muslin or gauze.

Finally, buy a stock pot. Besides its intended use in making broths and stocks that require large volumes of bones and vegetables, it will do double duty in the cooking of corn on the cob, the steaming of lobsters or puddings, and the sterilizing of jam jars, at least on an occasional basis. The ideal stock pot is a deep, heavy aluminum or stainless steel, double-handled pot that holds four gallons (16L) or more. It really is a must for chicken carcasses (though it is too deep to sauté in conveniently).

A tureen is not a necessary adjunct to soup-making, but it allows you to serve your soup from the dining table when you are eating family-style. It is a deep and shapely two-handled serving bowl with a lid that helps keep its contents warm. If you have attractive enameled pots, or Corning-type ware, these too can be used to serve the family, but on special occasions, when the soup is served from the sideboard, the tureen is essential.

DEFINITIONS

Soups range from basic stocks, vegetable or animal, through purées to full meals in a single bowl that are but a step removed from stews. The following is a list of the common soups with their sometimes overlapping definitions:

BROTH is a liquid in which meat or vegetables have been gently simmered. We tend to think of broth as clarified, but it need not be so. It is, however, strained of the meat or vegetables.

STOCK is a broth made of meat, fish, or vegetables and other aromatics—onions, garlic, ginger, or peppercorns, for example—which used to be kept simmering on the back of the stove and was replenished as needed. It can also be an extract of animal or vegetable materials used to enrich soups or sauces. For our purposes, stock will be the product of simmering meats, fish, and/or vegetables, and will be assumed to be of a normal edible strength unless otherwise specified. As with broths, stocks are strained of all solids before use.

CONSOMMÉ is a light colored, sparkling clear soup made from chicken, beef, or veal, and in some cases all three. It is almost always garnished, but has no bits of the original meat in it. Consommés can be served hot or cold.

BOUILLON is a darker, concentrated, clear soup, generally made from beef, although various other clear soups are sometimes called bouillons. The ubiquitous bouillon cube exists in chicken, beef, and vegetable flavors and has little to do with actual soup.

FISH FUMET is a fish stock made by boiling together a vegetable garnish and the head, bones, and skin of fish, augmented by shrimp, lobster, and crab shells, if available. As this production requires but 30 minutes of actual simmering time, it is neither necessary nor desirable to prepare and store it in advance.

CHOWDER is a thick, chunky soup of fish, meat, or vegetables to which milk has been added. Its name comes from *chaudière*, the French word for cauldron.

BISQUE, by comparison, is a rich, smoothly puréed cream soup based on shellfish, sometimes with added tomato purée.

GUMBO is a Southern meat and vegetable soup specialty whose defining ingredients are roux (page 125) and okra (the word "gumbo" is derived from an African word for okra).

POTAGE is French for a thick soup; it is at the root of our word "potagerie" ("herb and vegetable garden"). "A mess of pottage" is therefore presumably a thick soup from the bounty of the kitchen garden (when it is not in Scotland, where it is a bowl of oatmeal porridge), though it can contain other ingredients, too.

INGREDIENTS

The list of potential ingredients for soup include half of the produce and dairy sections of your local supermarket, a good portion of the meats and seafood counters, and certain canned goods, too. We will discuss rather the condition of your ingredients. In general, freshness is essential. The fresher the ingredients, the better the flavor, and the more they have to communicate to the soup. That said, their beauty is not terribly important. Bruises may be cut out with impunity and bad spots with care. And there are benefits to using slightly overripe vegetables, since their sugars are more complex and more easily impart flavor. Flavor is the key, so make sure that the bad spot in your tomato, for instance, hasn't affected the flavor of the whole fruit, which will then spoil the flavor of the whole soup.

In general, **FRESH PRODUCE** will contribute more flavor and texture to your soup than frozen; however, if your aim is to dress up a can of consommé, a supply of frozen vegetables can be a blessing. And as noted above, vegetables that are slightly past their prime have much to recommend them when making soup.

LEGUMES seem always and only to be available in a preserved state: indeed, one of their advantages is the variety of forms in which they are available. I try whenever possible to use dried legumes soaked overnight; my second choice is to cover the dried legumes with cold water, bring them to a boil, and let them stand tightly covered off the heat for an hour while other preparations go forward. Lastly, if time is really short, out comes the can opener; alas, the texture of the soup suffers by the use of canned legumes. Whatever method you choose, be sure to rinse the beans before adding them to the soup.

DRIED HERBS can be used in soups interchangeably with fresh in most cases, although the amounts differ: use $1/3$ to $1/2$ teaspoon of dried herbs to replace 2 to 3 teaspoons of fresh herbs. Exceptions to this assessment are dill, chervil, and parsley, whose flavor very nearly disappears when they are dried. The other side of this coin is the bay leaf, which is better dried than fresh. Try to use European or Turkish bay leaf instead of the California variety; this is not snobbery, for they are two different plants and the European (which is admittedly difficult to find in some parts of the world) makes for better bay flavor. Along these same lines, elephant garlic has a lovely mild flavor but does not impart the same savor when cooked as does the common garden variety. To release the flavor of whole sprigs of herbs, try rolling them gently between the palms of your hands before adding them to the soup; similarly, dried herbs may be helped along by bruising them between two spoons, in a mortar, or simply with the fingers.

"SALT AND PEPPER, to taste," "adjust seasoning to taste," and the like are instructions to be found throughout these recipes and everywhere in cookery around the world. For the purpose of flavoring soups, it matters little whether you use Kosher, sea, coarse, or normal table salt. Of course, there are various other reasons—religion, diet, health, availability—for using any one of these varieties, but none of them will affect the actual flavor of the recipe.

I am, however, a firm believer in the use of **FRESHLY GROUND PEPPERCORNS** whenever possible. Whole peppercorns keep their flavor longer than the jars of ground or cracked peppercorns, and with a pepper mill it is possible to control the coarseness of the grind, affecting the flavor, texture, and appearance of the end result. And yes, there is a difference in flavor between white and black peppercorns (the latter of which tend to have more bite).

Finally, a word about **CAYENNE**: throughout these recipes you will find references to "a pinch of cayenne." Although some of these soups are spicy hot, the pinch of cayenne in an otherwise mild soup is used to add another dimension—not heat but piquancy. It should evoke, "How interesting!" rather than a gasp and, "Spicy!"

TECHNIQUES

To discuss the "techniques" of soup-making is to assume that this age-old kitchen art might embrace some mysterious technology. Rather, there are a few fundamental points to keep in mind.

Start at the very beginning; that is, read the entire recipe. Assemble the necessary utensils. Clear the counter and do the dishes from your previous effort or meal. Get out all the ingredients so that there will be no unpleasant surprises in midstream. Check the yield of your recipe and perhaps write down alterations so that you don't halve or double some ingredients and not others. Finally, check not only the preparation time, but also the time necessary for the proper chilling of cold soups. These are all the most basic of injunctions, but things will go more smoothly if they are respected. I have been known to neglect one or more of these points and later regret it.

Soup is a happy ending for many of the tidbits in your refrigerator, both cooked and raw. Keep in mind, however, that if you are using leftovers in a soup they will add at best a point of interest, their flavors having already been fixed or carried away by the previous cooking. They will add little to the savory amalgamation that is your stock. Bits of steak, for instance, particularly if well done, might require bolstering by the addition of a soup bone, or even something as simple

as a little sautéed ground beef. My own freezer is full of old bones, cooked and raw, and of various pedigrees, awaiting a worthwhile end in a soupy concoction. If you become an ardent, daily soup-maker, you may find yourself saving the water used in cooking up the day's vegetables for tomorrow's soup.

Do consider how well the flavors of your ingredients blend. You may not want the flavor of parsnips or peas in your stock. Tasty as they are, they are sweet and their flavor permeates. It might be preferable to cook them separately and add them at the end of cooking. There are many cooking flavors that do not quite suit each other. This being said, soup is very forgiving by nature; feel free to substitute, using your judgment as to what goes with what.

To extract the maximum flavor from the ingredients in the soup pot, submerge the ingredients in cold water and bring very slowly to a boil—this process can take up to half an hour—then simmer for long periods. Needless to say, those ingredients will afterward have little left to recommend them either in flavor or texture, but you will have a pot full of delicious stock, to be used in future soups. Since some reduction of the liquid occurs with long cooking, salt should be used only sparingly at the outset and adjusted at the time of ultimate use.

By contrast, sautéing ingredients over high heat or dropping them into rapidly boiling liquid seals in their flavors. Therefore, if you sauté and then add water as a vehicle for simmering, you will have at best a thin soup with tasty morsels. It is for this reason that most recipes are based on a prepared stock or broth; the solid ingredients are then prepared with attention to optimal timing and methods for preserving flavor, texture, and appearance.

The longer your soup takes to cook, the more sensible it is to make large quantities. Though some soups don't reheat well at all, like the rich soups thickened with cream and egg yolks or those with potatoes, others may be frozen with impunity and kept for months, notably broths, stocks, and the vegetable purées based on them. The latter may be thawed and deliciously embroidered upon with the aforementioned bits of steak or even seafood.

By way of finishing touches, there are a few points to keep in mind:

• Alcohol is to be added just before serving; the soup must then be reheated to the point of steaming, but it must not boil.

• Generally speaking, soup should be served either piping hot, preferably in heated soup plates or bowls, or very well-chilled. One tends to think that fruit soups, or cucumber or gazpacho soups, which require little or no cooking, can be whipped up in a jiffy and made at the last minute. This is only half true: quick they may be, but you must allow 1½ to 2 hours for chilling. Room temperature is almost never the goal.

• Finally, there is the matter of serving quantities. A light first course should be about ½ to ¾ cup (125–188ml) of soup for each diner. As a main course, however, allow at least 1 cup (250ml) and probably more per person. Dessert soups are sometimes served in sherbet cups, requiring about ½ cup of soup, and sometimes in soup plates or bowls that

hold up to 1 cup. The lesser amount should be adequate, especially if accompanied by cookies or wafers.

CLARIFYING

As has been often mentioned above, most stocks are sufficiently clear for everyday use once they have been strained through a cloth. However, for that one occasion requiring sparkle, the method is as follows:

1. Cool the stock and remove as much fat as possible. Place the stock in a saucepan and set aside.

2. For each quart of stock, place 1 egg white and 2 tablespoons (20ml) of cold water in a small bowl and beat with a fork. Add this mixture to the stock along with the eggshells, crushed in pieces.

3. Bring slowly to a simmer, stirring constantly. The mixture will become milky and then the egg white will bind with the particles in the soup and hold

them in suspension. Reduce the heat as low as possible and let the stock cook for 20 minutes just below a simmer.

4. When the process is completed, line a colander or strainer with a cloth wrung out in hot water and strain out the eggshells and the suspended matter.

FINISHES AND THICKENERS

Purées are soups that are strained or blended and are naturally thickened in that process by their starchy components. Further thickening may, of course, be added, but in lesser amounts than for thinner soups.

Other thickeners must be added at the end of the cooking process, allowing additional time if necessary to cook the thickener itself. Flour requires about 5 minutes to eliminate its raw flavor; cornstarch requires about one minute;

quick-cooking tapioca takes 1 to 5 minutes, depending on how you are using it.

• **BEURRE MANIÉ** ("manipulated butter") consists of butter and flour rubbed together with the fingers, or, if the butter is sufficiently softened, mashed with a fork. Use one part butter with up to two parts flour, making sure the paste is perfectly smooth. This can also be accomplished in the following manner: melt the butter in a small saucepan. As soon as it's melted, turn off the heat and

incorporate the flour, stirring constantly. Then pour mixture into a small mold. Refrigerate to solidify. Beurre manié may be whisked directly into the hot soup; or if whisking is difficult because of the solid content of the soup, spoon off part of the liquid into the beurre manié, mix together thoroughly, then stir all back into the pot. Cook gently for about 5 minutes or until the thickening process halts. One tablespoon (15g) of beurre manié will thicken 2 to 3 cups (500–750ml) of soup.

• A similar binder for leguminous soups that tend to separate can be created by blending together one part melted butter with two parts flour. Stir in a small quantity of a suitable cold liquid (stock, water, or milk), then add to the hot soup. Simmer for about five minutes, or until thickened. One tablespoon (15g) of flour will thicken 2 to 3 cups (500–750ml) of soup.

• If your recipe or diet will not tolerate the extra butter, you may whisk together 1 tablespoon (15g) of flour with 2 table-spoons (30ml) of a suitable cold liquid. Dilute this paste with a little soup, blend in well, and return the flour mixture to the soup, again simmering about 5 min-utes longer.

• Roux is the last of the flour thickeners, and it comes in three shades. When you stir flour into melted butter and cook over low heat for 5 minutes, stirring constantly, the resulting whitish paste is called a **WHITE ROUX**; it is the basis for a white sauce or béchamel and may be used to thicken a cream sauce or velouté (that is, a béchamel made with stock instead of milk). Dilute carefully with a cold liquid to avoid lumps before adding to the soup. Since the flour is already cooked, the soup need only be returned to the simmering point.

The **BLOND ROUX** is made by the same method, but the flour and butter are cooked, constantly stirred, until a luxurious golden hue is achieved,

perhaps 15 to 20 minutes. This roux is used in velouté sauces and soups.

The king of the roux is the **BROWN ROUX**. A friend from Louisiana tells us that you must cook a brown roux for at least 45 minutes over very low heat, stirring almost constantly, so pull up a stool and equip yourself with a book. Make a good quantity—this roux keeps forever in the freezer, and perhaps half as long in the refrigerator—because in addition to thickening soups, it is also much-used in sauces. The proportions are as above, one part fat to two parts flour, but the fat can be butter, oil, drippings, or the fat from your stock pot. The resulting thickener will of course flavor your soup, so choose your fat with care. The latter half of the cooking time may be done in a moderate oven, but you must still stir frequently to provide an even browning. Using either method, the roux should be a deep nut-brown in color; be careful not to scorch it

• **VARIOUS GRAINS**, such as barley, rice, and oatmeal, lend themselves well to the thickening of soups. These may be added for the last hour or so of cooking, the rule of thumb for amounts being 1 tablespoon (15g) per 3 cups (750ml) of liquid used in making the soup. If you are using rice as an ingredient and not just as a thickener, add it 30 minutes before serving, as it will continue to absorb liquid and thicken the soup beyond your wildest

expectations. Simmer for 30 minutes, or the time specified in the recipe, and serve at once.

• Quick-cooking **TAPIOCA** may be used for a thickener in the proportion of 2 teaspoons (10g) to 3 cups (750ml) of liquid. Tapioca does not require long cooking and may be used to thicken fruit soups with just a small amount of cooking time after addition.

• Some soups may be thickened by the addition of $1/2$ cup (125g) of grated or finely chopped **RAW POTATO** for every three cups (750ml) of soup; allow 15 or 20 minutes additional cook-ing time when using this method.

• **CORNSTARCH** is a clear thick-ening agent often used in oriental soups, and sometimes in fruit soups. It must be stirred into cold water just before adding it to the soup; 4 teaspoons (20g) of cornstarch to 3 tablespoons (45ml) of water will thicken about 2 cups (500ml) of soup.

• **EGG YOLK** may be added to thicken milk or cream-based soups just before serving. Beat the egg yolk with 1 tablespoon (15ml) or so of milk, cream, or flavoring wine. Add a bit of hot soup to the egg; mix well, then return the mixture to the soup, stirring con-stantly. Heat and stir carefully; to avoid curdling, do not allow the soup to boil. If you must reheat such a soup, do it in the top of a double-boiler over hot water.

INDEX